Pearson Scott Foresman
Writing Rubrics and Anchor Papers

Grade 3

Glenview, Illinois
Boston, Massachusetts
Chandler, Arizona
Upper Saddle River, New Jersey

ISBN-13: 978-0-328-47654-1
ISBN-10:   0-328-47654-4

9 10 V031 15 14 13 12

Contents

Writing Models

Weekly Rubrics

Support for Writing

Suggestions for Using This Book

This book is most effective when used in conjunction with the weekly writing lessons and unit writing process lessons in Scott Foresman's *Reading Street*. Rubrics and anchor papers can be copied and distributed or made into transparencies. Here are some ways to use the materials.

- Distribute copies of page v to students. Work through the explanations of traits with the class to develop background for discussing scores.

- Display one-by-one the four models for a given mode in order (starting with Score 1 or Score 4). Work through the commentaries that appear along with the models to illustrate how each got its score.

- After students become proficient with determining scores, distribute copies of writing models from this book with the scores screened out. Work with students to arrive at scores.

- Display a model that is Score 1. Work with students to improve the model.

- Display the rubric for the type of writing you are teaching. Have students use the rubric to evaluate their own writing.

- Distribute copies of the Self-Evaluation Guide on page vi. Have students use this guide to evaluate their work.

Tips for Teaching and Evaluating Writing

- Choose one writing trait to emphasize each week. Appoint a team of students for each trait. Have them find their trait in selections they read and in their own writing and present their findings to the class.

- Read short passages from literature (for example, a tall tale) and from other content areas (for example, a science text). Point out how writer's purpose determines voice, word choice, and style.

- Remember that a writer may be more proficient in one trait than in another. To arrive at a score, evaluators must weigh proficiency in all traits.

- Tell students that when they evaluate their own writing, assigning a score of 3, 2, or even 1 does not necessarily indicate a failure. The ability to identify areas for improvement in future writing is a valuable skill.

- Encourage students to think of themselves as writers. Alert them that subjects, words, and ideas are everywhere. Suggest they keep a notebook handy to record material, such as overheard conversations, sentences from their reading, and vivid words they encounter.

- Join students as they write. Share your own writing with them and ask for their feedback on your work.

- Model constructive ways of giving feedback on writing. (*Words such as* pounce *and* swat *give me a good picture of your cat. You said her name is Boots. How did she get that name? You mentioned that she has a favorite place to sleep. Could you describe it?*)

Writing Traits

Traits

- Focus/Ideas
- Organization
- Voice
- Word Choice
- Sentences
- Conventions

- **Focus/Ideas** refers to the main purpose for writing and the details that make the subject clear and interesting. It includes development of ideas through support and elaboration.

- **Organization** refers to the overall structure that guides readers through a piece of writing. Within that structure, transitions show how ideas, sentences, and paragraphs are connected.

- **Voice** shows the writer's unique personality and establishes a connection between writer and reader. Voice, which contributes to style, should be suited to the audience and the purpose for writing.

- **Word Choice** is the use of precise, vivid words to communicate effectively and naturally. It helps create style through the use of specific nouns, lively verbs and adjectives, and accurate, well-placed modifiers.

- **Sentences** covers strong, well-built sentences that vary in length and type. Skillfully written sentences have pleasing rhythms and flow fluently.

- **Conventions** refers to mechanical correctness and includes grammar, usage, spelling, punctuation, capitalization, and paragraphing.

Self-Evaluation Guide

Name _____

Name of Writing Product _____

Directions Review your final draft. Then rate yourself on a scale from 4 to 1 (4 is a top score) on each writing trait. After you fill out the chart, answer the questions.

Writing Traits	4	3	2	1
Focus/Ideas				
Organization				
Voice				
Word Choice				
Sentences				
Conventions				

1. What is the best part of this piece of writing? Why do you think so?

   _____

   _____

   _____

2. Write one thing you would change about this piece of writing if you had the chance to write it again.

   _____

   _____

   _____

   _____

Writing Models

PROMPT

Write about a time you worked hard for something you wanted. Tell what you wanted, why you wanted it, and what you did to get it.

Rubric	4	3	2	1
Focus/Ideas	Personal narrative well focused and developed with many supporting details	Personal narrative generally focused and developed with supporting details	Personal narrative often off topic; lacks enough supporting details	Personal narrative lacking focus or sufficient information
Organization	Clear sequence of events with time-order words	Reasonably clear sequence with one or two lapses	Confused sequence of events	No attempt to sequence events, or sequence is incoherent
Voice	Sincere, engaging, and unique voice	Pleasant voice but not compelling or unique	No clear, original voice	Uninvolved or indifferent
Word Choice	Vivid descriptive words that show instead of tell	Some vivid words that show instead of tell	Few vivid words that show instead of tell	No attempt to show instead of tell
Sentences	Clear sentences, variety of types	Mostly clear sentences with some variety	Some sentences unclear; little or no variety	Incoherent sentences, or only short, choppy sentences
Conventions	Few, if any, errors	Several minor errors	Frequent errors that detract from meaning	Serious errors that prevent understanding

Eye of The Tiger

"Score! The Eagles win the game!" yelled the referee. And, that my friend was another loss for the Tigers.

I play soccer every Saturday for the Tigers. We had lost the last four games in a row, making this the beginning of the worst soccer season ever. I wanted to feel the triumph of at least one win this season. So, I knew something had to change, and with only six games left I had to think of something quick.

First, I knew I would need a little spending money—a little more than usual—so I did extra chores around the house to increase my allowance. I used every penny of it to buy my very own soccer ball so that I could practice every day after I finished my homework. After that, I bought a set of orange cones to help me with my dribble drills. Then I asked my older brother, who is a great soccer player, to come outside and give me some pointers. With his help, my footwork was coming along nicely. On a Friday night, the night before our next game, I invited my soccer teammates over to my house for a sleepover. My plan was to get them psyched and ready to win. We watched a movie about some

Continued on next page

kids who play soccer. I thought my teammates would be inspired by this movie since it was about a not so great soccer team like ours who struggle and never seem to win. But they practice really hard and start to work together as a team. They make it all the way to the championship game. I don't want to spoil the ending, but let's just say we were ready to win our game.

It was game time. We had the ball. Dribble. Dribble. Pass. I scored the winning goal. The final score was 4-2. We did it! We won! We are the Tigers! Now for the rest of the season.

Score 4

This is an excellent response to the writing task. The personal narrative focuses on how the writer worked hard for something he wanted. The writing is well developed with lots of details; the sequence of events is clear, and time-order words are used. The writer is involved and expresses feelings clearly. Words such as *triumph, inspired,* and *struggle,* as well as the description of the scoring of the final pass, create picture and mood. Sentences are well constructed and include a variety of types. Incorrect comma placement in the second sentence does not interfere with the writer's meaning.

My New Bike

My bike and I had changed over the past two years. I weighed 15 pounds more and was almost a half-foot taller. My bike's frame was scratched, and the front fender was dented from hitting the tree in front of my house. Both tires were wobbly, and I looked funny when I rode it. Because I wobbled too.

This spring it was time to take action! Dad and me went to the Big Wheel to check out bikes. I saw a bright-red mountain bike. It was the shiniest bike I had ever seen! It had five gears and super-tread tires. That bike was just my size, and I didn't have to hunker over to ride it like with the old bike. I knew that it was the bike for me!

To earn money for the bike, I did jobs for people in my neighborhood. I passed out a flyer that listed all the things I could do. And the amount I charged. I mowed my next-door neighbor's grass, sorted newspapers for recycling, and washed cars. Soon neighbors started calling me to do work. Mr. Vargas said, "Cal, my place has never looked so good." That made me proud.

By August, I had enough money to buy the bike. Now I ride every day.

Continued on next page

Score 3

The narrative is elaborated with many telling details, and with one exception, is related in time order. The writer's voice is pleasant and interested. Word choice *(dented, wobbly, super-tread, hunker)* is colorful and specific. Two sentence fragments and a pronoun error *(Dad and me went…)* mar an otherwise strong narrative.

How I Got a Electric Piano

I always wanted a electric piano. I wanted the electric piano because I seen this movie called Freaky Friday. It's about girls who play music. I watched another movie called Mozart. It's about a guy that plays piano. I thought it would be cool to get a electric piano. I also watched a movie that was about kids that put on a musical at their school. I saw that movie a lot of times.

I ask my mom and dad about getting a piano. They said yes, but had to work for it. I would have to wash 11 windows and 3 mirrors plus wash the car which wasn't so easy. I started to work the day after that. I jumped up and down saying yay.

I scrubbed the windows and mirrors. It was really hard work. I cleaned the windows and mirrors and started to clean our black minivan. That was hard work too. It was sunny outside. I wanted to ride my bike or play with my friends.

Continued on next page

> I finally got my electric piano. It was black, white, red, blue, green, and gray. My sister taught me how to play songs. I was so happy to get my piano.

Score 2

The narrative describes a goal, but sometimes veers off topic and lacks sufficient supporting details. The order in which events happens is sometimes unclear or confused. Word choice, (with the exception of *black minivan*) is general and does not help readers paint a picture. Language is sometimes informal *(guy, cool)*. Most sentences begin with *I*. Grammatical and usage errors *(a electric, I seen, kids that)*, along with a number of punctuation errors, provide notable distractions.

Perpetual Motion

I wanted to play Perpetual Motion for my violin recital becuse of the fact that its my favrit song and I had to work at it and practice a lot. I had to play it at least 7 times a day for a long time becuse I worked hard for it I got to play it for my recital. I was happy I got to play it for my recital. When I finly acheved my gool I was prowd of myself.

Continued on next page

Score 1

This narrative lacks development and supporting details. Sentences are stringy and overconnected with *and* and *because ("becuse")*. Wordiness (for example, *becuse of the fact that*), lack of punctuation in the title of a song, and many spelling errors seriously detract from the writing. There is no paragraph indentation.

PROMPT

Write about how you can make or do something in a few simple steps.

Rubric	4	3	2	1
Focus/Ideas	How-to report well focused and fully developed	How-to report generally focused and developed	How-to report strays from topic or lacks necessary details	How-to report lacking focus or having sufficient information
Organization	Sequence of steps clear and easy to follow	Sequence of steps fairly clear	Sequence of steps confused	Incoherent sequence or no sequence
Voice	Knowledgeable, enthusiastic voice	Voice trustworthy but not compelling or unique	No clear, original voice	Uninvolved or indifferent
Word Choice	Effective use of vivid words and time-order words	Some vivid words; some time-order words	Few vivid words, few or no time-order words	Incorrect or limited word choice
Sentences	Clear sentences, uses commands	Mostly clear sentences; uses some commands	Many unclear sentences; uses no commands	Incoherent sentences, or only short, choppy sentences
Conventions	Few, if any, errors	Several minor errors	Frequent errors	Many errors that detract from the writing

How to Make a Bird Feeder

Do you like to watch birds in your yard during the winter? You can help birds and have fun too by making a bird feeder. I will tell you how to make a bird feeder that many birds will like.

For this bird feeder, you will need a pine cone, a long string, peanut butter, margarine, and birdseed. First, tie the string to the top of the pine cone. Second, mix some peanut butter and margarine together. Your mixture should contain one-half peanut butter and one-half margarine. Next, spread this sticky mixture all over the pine cone. Put some birdseed on a plate. Then roll the pine cone around so that birdseed sticks all over it. Put the pine cone in the freezer for an hour or so. Finally, hang the pine cone on a tree branch outside your house. Now you can see how many different kinds of birds live in your neighborhood.

Continued on next page

Score 4

This report is well focused and developed with necessary details. It begins with an introduction that states the topic and attracts interest. Steps are in a clear sequence, signaled by the time-order words *first, second, next, then,* and *finally*. The writer expresses interest in the activity and knowledge of the steps involved. Precise verbs such as *spread* and *hang* make information clear. Sentences are varied. There is good control of conventions.

How to Make an Art Rubbing

The materials for a great art project are at your fingertips. All you need are some objects with interesting shapes. Everyone has items in their drawers or pockets such as paper clips, coins, keys, and combs. Collect a few of these. Get some crayons and paper. I will show you the nesessary steps to make an unusual art rubbing. First, put a coin on a flat table. Then place a peice of thin paper on top of the coin. Hold the paper's edges with one hand so it doesn't crumple. Rub the side of a crayon over the paper. You will see that a design appears on the paper. Next try an object with a different shape like a key. Rub each object on several different areas of the page to form letters, borders, and other shapes. Use many colors to make bright patterns. You can use your artwork to make greeting cards or to decorate the borders of stories and poems that you write.

Continued on next page

Score 3

Steps are clear in this how-to report, although the introduction (first six sentences) should be a separate paragraph. Voice is believable and straightforward, but not unique. Some vivid and time-order words are used. Most sentences are clear and varied and use commands. A few minor spelling and conventions errors do not detract from the writing.

How to Walk A Dog

Step 1: Find the leash.

Step 2: Attach leash to dogs collar

Step 3: Take dog to the door

Step 4: Walk the dog.

Step 5: Walk dog until needed exersise has been fulfilled

Step 6: Return dog home

Step 7: Return leash to proper place of storage

Continued on next page

Score 2

The steps in this how-to report are clear, but are written as a list, not a report. Voice is mechanical and flat. Two vivid words *(fulfilled, proper)* and no time-order words, though numbered list clearly shows the order in which steps are to be completed. Commands are used, though few complete sentences are included. Missing apostrophe in *dogs* in step 2 and a misspelled word in step 5 *(exersise)*, along with numerous incomplete sentences, detract somewhat from writing.

How to Tie a Knot

I learnt how to tie a knot in a rope. You cross the two
ends of the rope over make a loop and you stick it
through and pull the ends and your done.

Continued on next page

Score 1

Information is confusing and steps are not isolated in this how-to. There are no time-order words. The final "sentence" is a run-on that is actually three sentences. There are two spelling errors *(learnt, your* for *you're)*. There is no paragraph indentation.

PROMPT ▶ Write about how something that happens in nature is the effect of one or more causes.

Rubric	4	3	2	1
Focus/Ideas	Cause-and-effect essay well focused with many supporting facts and details	Cause-and-effect essay generally focused; some supporting facts and details	Cause-and-effect essay poorly focused; few supporting facts and details	Cause-and-effect essay lacking focus or sufficient supporting facts and details
Organization	States central idea; organized logically in paragraphs; has concluding statement	States central idea; organized in paragraphs; has concluding statement	Central idea not clearly stated; some paragraphs; no concluding statement	Not organized
Voice	Conversational and informed voice	Engaging voice but lacks expertise	Uncertain voice	Dull writing with no clear voice
Word Choice	Vivid words; uses cause-and-effect words correctly	Mostly vivid words; some cause-and-effect words	Mostly dull words; few cause-and-effect words	No vivid words or cause-and-effect words
Sentences	Clear sentences; variety of types and structures	Sentences mostly clear and varied	Some sentences unclear; little variety	Incoherent or unvaried sentences
Conventions	Few, if any, errors	Several minor errors	Frequent errors that detract from writing	Serious errors that hamper understanding

Seasons

There are four seasons in a year. In most places in the united states, the weather in summer is really different from the weather in winter. Let me explain why.

The Earth orbits around the sun, which warms it. The Earth also rotates on an axis. The axis isn't straight up and down. It is on an angle. Because of the angle, we get more daylight in the summer and less daylight in the winter.

When there is more daylight, that means there is more sun to keep Earth warm. When Earth is warm, it causes plants to grow. This is what happens in spring and summer.

When there is less daylight, there is less sun to keep Earth warm. When Earth cools down, the effect is that trees shed of their leaves, and many plants die because it is too cold. This is what happens in fall and winter.

And that is why Earth has seasons.

Continued on next page

Score 4

This essay is focused on seasons, and includes explanations, supporting details, and a conclusion. Voice is interested and informed. The writer uses a number of specific words *(orbits, rotates, axis, angle, shed)*, and includes cause-and-effect words appropriately. Sentences are varied. There is one capitalization error *(united states)* that does not detract from the essay.

Rain Forests

Rain forests are important to everyone in the world! We have to make sure that the rain forests survive!

First, there are many animals and bugs that live in the rain forest. Scientists keep finding more over time. If the rain forest is gone the effect is that those animals and bugs might become extinct.

Next, there are lots of important things like medecine that are made with plants that come from the rain forest. When the rain forest is cut down, there aren't as many of those plants to make medecine. The effect is that some people could die because there isn't medecine for them.

Last rain forests are full of thousands and thousands of trees. These trees make oxygen that people and animals need to live. More oxygen is produced in the rain forests than anywhere else on Earth! If there are less trees, the cause is that there won't be as much oxygen being made. If this keeps happening, there won't be enough oxygen for everyone.

People need to take care of the rain forest so that these things don't happen!

Continued on next page

Score 3

This essay is generally focused on causes and effects related to rain forests and provides some clear supporting details and a brief conclusion. Voice is concerned and involved. Some cause-and-effect words are included, and sentences are generally varied. A few minor punctuation errors and a consistently misspelled word (*medecine*), do little to distract from the writing.

Earthquakes

When two plates underneath the surface of the Earth crash, the ground shakes and rumbles. This is called an earthquake.

Some of the worst earthquakes the world has seen have nocked over billdings and started fires. And if you live near the ocean and a earthquake happens your in big trouble because a tsumamie is coming your way. One of the biggest earthquiks was Sanfransican earthquake, wich knocked down buildings causing fires. After the horrible quake, many people died, and the people that lived had problems like there house blown to bits, in flames, or both.

Continued on next page

Score 2

This essay is focused on earthquakes, but provides little information about their causes or effects. Some sentences stray from the focus. There are few cause-and-effect words. There is some sentence variation, but numerous spelling, punctuation, and capitalization errors detract from the writing.

It's a Beautiful Thing!

The butterfly is a beautiful thing! A butterfly looks very different in each part of it's life cycle. First, the butterfly lays an egg, the egg then turns into a caterpiller. The caterpiller then turns into a pupa. After that the beautiful butterfly is produced. In its life cycle the butterfly is many different shapes, first it is round then it is long and has an interesting pattern. It becomes a beautiful butterfly.

Continued on next page

Score 1

This essay does not appropriately address the prompt. It discusses stages of
a butterfly's life cycle, but does not point out any specific causes or effects.
A misspelled word *(caterpiller)* and a run-on sentence also contribute to the
low score.

PROMPT ▶ **Write about a problem in your school or community and how that problem might be solved.**

Rubric	4	3	2	1
Focus/Ideas	Problem-solution essay well focused on one problem and solution	Problem-solution essay generally focused on one problem and solution	Problem-solution essay poorly focused; unclear problem and solution	Problem-solution essay lacking focus; no problem and/or solution
Organization	Well organized; clear topic sentence, body, concluding statement	Organized, with topic sentence, body, concluding statement	Lacking clear topic sentence, body, concluding statement	Not organized
Voice	Knowledgeable, confident voice	Generally knowledgeable and convincing	Uncertain voice	No clear voice
Word Choice	Uses descriptive and persuasive words effectively	Uses some descriptive and persuasive words	Few descriptive or persuasive words	No descriptive or persuasive words
Sentences	Clear, logical sentences	Reasonably clear, logical sentences	Choppy sentences with lapses in logic	Fragments or run-on sentences
Conventions	Few, if any, errors	Several minor errors	Frequent errors	Errors that hamper understanding

Clean It Up!

One big problem in my community is dirty vacant lots. Vacant lots are a problem because they are dirty and no one really uses them.

Vacant lots always seem to have garbage in them. Sometimes garbage gets blown into the lots by the wind. Some other garbage is left there by people. No one lives there, so no one cleans up the garbage.

Vacant lots never really get used. Oh, sometimes people walk through them, but otherwise they just sit there with nothing going on.

I think I have a good solution for the problem. I think people in the community should work together to clean up the lots and take care of them. If we get rid of the garbage and plant grass and other beautiful plants, the vacant lots will look fantastic! If the lots are cleaned up, people will be able to use them for many different activities. Adults can plant gardens so that they have more food to eat or pretty flowers to look at. Kids can use the lots to play games like baseball and statue.

Continued on next page

I think that if we clean up the vacant lots, they will not be a problem any more. People will be happier and have nicer lots to look at. Don't you think this is a great solution?

Score 4

This essay is focused on one problem and solution. The writer includes a topic sentence, body, and concluding statement. Voice is confident, knowledgeable, and enthusiastic. The writer uses descriptive and persuasive words (*dirty, blown, beautiful, fantastic, pretty, happier, nicer*) to get her point across. Sentences are varied and complete. There is excellent control of conventions.

Let's Stay Healthy

The problem in my comunity is that the flue is going around and many people are getting sick. My solution to this problem is to make sure people know what to do so they don't get sick.

Sick people should try to avoid spreding their germs to other people. They should stay home and get better. But if you go to school anyway, cover your mouth when you cough or sneeze. Also wash your hands often so that you don't spread germs around.

If you aren't sick already you should avoid people that are sick and you should wash your hands a lot. This helps you get rid of germs you might get before they make you sick. Also, use hand sanitizer throughout the day. Things that lots of different people use should be sanitized too. Like computer keyboards, door handles, and telephones. And disinfeckt other things that lots of people touch.

If everyone does all these things, there won't be lots of people that get sick, and everyone will be a lot happier!

Continued on next page

Score 3

This essay is focused on one problem and one basic solution. It has a clear organization including topic sentences with supporting details and a concluding statement. Voice is knowledgeable and informed, and the writer uses specific words and phrases *(cover your mouth, avoid, wash your hands, sanitizer)* to get the point across. There is a sentence fragment in paragraph three. Conventions errors include misspellings *(comunity, flue, spreding, disinfeckt)* and sentences with missing commas.

Stray dogs are a problem in our community. stray dogs might carry rabies. Stray dogs might bit to. Stray animals are the real problem because dogs can get in your garbage and nock your garbage out. And dogs run across the road and get cars into acsidents.

I think I know how to solve the problem in too solutions: Take the dogs to all the schools and let the kids take them home if they want to. Put up posters around the community. And that is my solution.

Continued on next page

Score 2

This essay focuses on one problem, but it does not include a topic sentence or concluding statement. The writer is involved in the subject, but uses few persuasive words to communicate his message. The writer's solution about putting up posters is undeveloped. Misspellings *(to* for *too, nock, acsidents, too* for *two),* a sentence lacking capitalization, and sentences with awkward wording also contribute to the low score.

Speed Limit

I have a few ideas to fix the problem. first is to make the signs bigger, second idea is to change the color of the signs from white to orange and last but not lest is to hire more police. If the signs are larger and orange people obey and make my neigborhood a safer place.

Continued on next page

Score 1

This essay is poorly focused and states the apparent problem only in the title. Pervasive errors in sentence construction and conventions seriously detract from the essay and account for the low score.

PROMPT > Write to persuade your parents to let you travel to another country, dress in a special way, or eat a particular food.

Rubric	4	3	2	1
Focus/Ideas	Well-focused essay; clear position	Generally focused essay; clear position	Essay lacking focus; unclear position	Essay without focus; no clear position
Organization	Supporting details given in order of importance	Supporting details given in fairly clear order	Supporting details given in confused order	No order; no supporting details
Voice	Sincere, persuasive voice	Voice somewhat sincere, persuasive	No clear, persuasive voice	Uninvolved or indifferent
Word Choice	Uses strong persuasive words to make reasons convincing	Uses some persuasive words	Uses few persuasive words	No attempt to use persuasive words
Sentences	Variety of strong, clear sentences	Mostly clear sentences; some variety	Little or no variety; some unclear sentences	Incoherent sentences or short, choppy sentences
Conventions	Few, if any, errors	Some minor errors	Many errors	Numerous serious errors

Mom, thanks for letting me invite Danny and Josh over tonight. Now I have another special favor to ask. Can we make pizza?

Our teacher, Mr. Lorenzo, gave us a great recipe for pizza. First you make the dough and roll it out until it is very flat. Then you put tomato sauce and different toppings on the dough. I would like to put cheese, sausage, mushrooms, peppers, and olives on our pizza. I will help you shop for ingredients. It will be fun and creative to make our own pizza. We will clean up the kitchen when we are done. It will be safe because I know you will help us with the oven. The pizza will be delicious. The best thing about the pizza is that it is full of nourishing things like cheese and vegetables. This will be a neat project that will be lots of fun and good for us. Please tell me that you will say yes!

Continued on next page

Score 4

Essay stays focused on the topic. Writer organizes reasons in order of importance. Writer's personality and persuasive abilities are evident. Words such as *great, creative, safe,* and *best* are convincing. Sentences are of varied lengths and kinds, including a question and an exclamation. Writer has good control of conventions.

Mom and Dad, I would like your permission to go to Nicaragua because my grandma was born there. I would like to go over there to better understand my heritage and my traditions and the Spanish community of Nicaragua. Of course, I could learn to cook the traditional foods, beans and rice that is called "gallo pinto." I want to learn more Spanish from their schools for Spanish speaking. I would like to learn the traditional dances that they do at festivals, and I would be able to wear the Nicaraguan dresses just like them. Over there they have the big lady they called the "gigantona" and her little brother "Pepe." If I went to Nicaragua I would be able to see them. I could also go to the beach everyday and I would be able to go on the boat with Nanita. By the way, I can call you everyday so you know everything is fine. If I go I can make art for everyone and send you pictures. So please, Mom and Dad, let me go. It would be a great experence for me and I would get to see my grandmother.

Continued on next page

Score 3

This essay is generally well organized around a number of persuasive reasons. The writer takes a clear position and does not stray from it. Most supporting reasons are given in clear order, and voice is sincere and genuine. Persuasive words and phrases are used. There is some variety in sentence structure, though many sentences begin with "I". Some minor grammatical, punctuation, and spelling errors do little to distract from the writing.

Please!

One day I asked my mom if I could have bagel pizzas everyday. But she said no so I had to convince her. I told her that they were my favorite and I liked the crust, the cheese was yummy and the sauce was warm. She still said no.

Next I tried to tell her they were healthy. They were easy to heat up because it only took 10 minutes. I never get tired of them. She still doubted my plans. I'll try one more time. Then I said please and she said yes for the first time.

Continued on next page

Score 2

The writer's position is clear, but not well supported. Rather than writing to try to convince a parent to do something, the writer has written about having already tried to do so. A few vivid and persuasive words are included *(favorite, yummy, healthy)*. There is some sentence variety, though the last sentence is a run-on. Many errors in punctuation detract from the writing.

Continued on next page

Me and my complex Wants

Daddy can I have a jet that can go 1,200 miles per hour? And in the insides of it there would be jet packs, food, a pool, and a jakusie, and servants to do all the dirty work please? No wey. because that would cost millions of dollars. Pwease I said in my baby voice. No. Yes. No. Yes and that went on between me and him for a while. But daddy got tired of me and sent me to my room. The End.

Continued on next page

Score 1

This response does not appropriately address the prompt. Errors in conventions seriously detract from this essay. Writer does not indent the paragraph, and errors in punctuation, capitalization, and spelling, along with sentence fragments, account for the low score.

PROMPT Write about a monument or statue in the United States that stands for freedom. Use sources such as books, interviews, online searches, and surveys.

Rubric	4	3	2	1
Focus/Ideas	Well-focused report with one clear topic	Generally focused report with clear topic	Report lacking focus; unclear topic	Report with no focus or clear topic
Organization	Paragraphs with strong topic and detail sentences	Most paragraphs have topic and detail sentences	Few paragraphs with topic and detail sentences	Not organized in paragraphs; no topic sentences
Voice	Interested, informed voice	Voice somewhat interested, informed	Vaguely interested voice	Uninterested or uninformed voice
Word Choice	Evidence of paraphrasing	Some evidence of paraphrasing	Paraphrasing attempted	No paraphrasing
Sentences	Varied, well-constructed simple, complex, and compound sentences	Well-constructed sentences, some variety	Some unclear sentences; little variety	Fragments and run-ons, no variety
Conventions	Few, if any, errors	Some minor errors	Errors that detract from writing	Serious errors that prevent understanding

Continued on next page

A Memorial

Have you ever wondered about the Lincoln Memorial? The Lincoln Memorial represents our 16th President – Abraham Lincoln. It is located in Washington, D.C.

The Lincoln Memorial represents freedom because President Lincoln freed the slaves to bring the country together. He believed in equality for all Americans.

The memorial is made of marble and was built on the National Mall. It is rectangular and has 36 columns. Each column stands for one of the 36 states in the United States when Lincoln was President. The Lincoln Memorial was dedicated by William Howard Taft on May 30, 1922. The architect was Henry Bacon. The statue of Abraham Lincoln was sculpted by Daniel C. French.

There were famous speeches held at the Lincoln Memorial. One example was the "I Have a Dream" speech by Dr. Martin Luther King, Jr., who also had the same vision as Lincoln. This is another reason I believe the memorial represents freedom.

Continued on next page

So if you ever have the chance to visit the Lincoln Memorial, remember it is more than just a building with a statue inside. It is a symbol of freedom and what this country went through so all its people could become free.

Score 4

This research report consists of several well-constructed paragraphs with topic sentences, many supporting details, and a conclusion. The writer shows thoughtfulness, originality, and thoroughness of research. The supporting information demonstrates evidence of paraphrasing through specific details *(dedicated by William Howard Taft on May 30, 1922)*. Sentences are well-constructed and include a combination of simple, complex, and compound sentences. There is good control of conventions.

The Statue of Liberty

The Statue of Liberty symbolizes freedom and was a gift from the people of France. It represents the friendship of the United States and France during the American Revolution. It is a symbol of democracy around the world. It's copper plating alone weighs a whopping sixty-two thousand pounds! From the ground to the end of the torch is three hundred and five feet one inch long. It was designed by Frederick-Auguste Bartholdi who gave the statue a seven point crown. Each point stands for the seven continents and seas. The skeletal frame was created by Alexander Gustave Eiffel, and the statue was completed in France in July 1884.

The Statue of Liberty arrived in the United States in June 1885. It was first cared for by the lighthouse board, then the war department, and finally the national park service in 1993. The attacks of September 11th, 2001 resulted in the closing of Liberty Island for 100 days, but even after the island was reopened to visitors, the statue remained closed until August 3rd, 2004. But people cannot go high up into the crown. For now, they are only allowed to go to the top of the pedestal.

Continued on next page

Score 3

This report has a clear topic and is focused and generally well supported with facts. The writer is engaged and interested in the topic. There is evidence of paraphrasing from sources *(cared for by the lighthouse board, then the war department, and finally the national park service; statue remained closed until August 3rd, 2004)*. Most sentences are varied and well constructed, but occasionally flow a bit awkwardly *(It is a symbol of democracy around the world. It's copper plating alone weighs a whopping sixty-two thousand pounds!)*. Some minor errors in capitalization and punctuation and one run-on sentence do not detract from the writing.

The Liberty Bell

One day in 1751, America ordered the Liberty bell from England. The bell is a symbol of freedom. The bell was first rang when they announced America's independence from Great Britan and it cracked. In 1751, The State House in Philadelphia needed a new bell. When it arrived people wanted to hear it. They pulled the clapper. Then it rang once then cracked.

After all these years, the bell survived three cracks! Now it is kept near independence Hall. The bell is struck to Honor Americas's Freedom.

Continued on next page

Score 2

This report has a clear topic, but the focus is sometimes unclear and is lacking sufficient supporting details. There is some evidence of an interested voice *(After all these years, the bell survived three cracks!)*. There is evidence of paraphrasing *(In 1751, The State House in Philadelphia needed…)*. The report shows some variety in sentence lengths and types. A number of errors in punctuation and spelling, as well as a error in tense *(bell was first rang)*, and an incorrect possessive *(Americas's)* detract from the report.

The Lincoln Memorial

The Lincoln Memorial is exactly 80 feet tall 189 feet long and 118 feet wide. It tock 7 years to build the Lincoln Memorial. The stacheu of Lincoln is 19 feet tall. The Lincoln Monumint was built to look like a Greeck tempel. The Lincoln memorial is importin because Lincoln was a very importin percin because he fred the Slaves and brung peace to the US. On one of the walls in the monumint thir's a panting called Emancipation and it's a panting of an agnel and its freeing a slave. And the stacheu of Lincoln faces the Washington monumint.

Continued on next page

Score 1

Serious and pervasive errors repeatedly detract the reader. Misspellings, incorrect capitalization, and an incorrect verb form *(brung)* indicate a poor understanding of conventions. In addition, many sentences are wordy, stringy, or overconnected with *and* or *because*.

Weekly Rubrics

NARRATIVE POEM

Rubric	6	5	4	3	2	1
Focus/Ideas	Vivid narration with well-chosen supporting details	Fairly vivid narrative with some details	Reasonably clear narrative with few details	Sometimes engaging narrative; needs more details	Few details and/or lack of focus in narrative	Not a narrative; lacks clarity and development
Organization	Uses lines and stanzas with clear sequence of events	Uses some lines and stanzas; can follow sequence	Reasonable organization of lines and stanzas	Some organization of lines and stanzas; sequence of events fairly unclear	No lines or stanzas; sequence of events not clear	No lines, stanzas, or sequence of events
Voice	Excellent sense of writer's attitude toward topic; strongly engages audience and speaks directly to them	Clear sense of how writer feels and thinks; engages audience	Some sense of how writer feels and thinks; somewhat engages audience	Attempts to show how writer feels and thinks; attempts to engage audience	Limited sense of how writer feels and thinks; weak attempt to engage audience	No sense of how writer feels and thinks about topic; no attempt to engage audience
Word Choice	Vivid style created by use of exact nouns, strong verbs, exciting adjectives, and clear figurative language	Clear style created by strong, precise words	Some style created by strong, precise words	Some style created by mix of general and specific words	Little style created by general terms; some lack of clarity	Word choice vague or incorrect
Sentences	Clear, interesting, unique sentences	Clear sentences	Some clear sentences; some variety	Few clear sentences; little variety	Very few clear sentences; no variety	Most sentences unclear; no variety of sentence structure
Conventions	Excellent control; few or no sentence errors	Good control; few sentence errors	Fair control; some errors	Limited control; some serious sentence errors	Weak control; several serious errors	Many serious sentence errors that affect meaning

Rubric	5	4	3	2	1
Focus/Ideas	Vivid narration with well-chosen supporting details	Fairly vivid narrative with some details	Reasonably clear narrative with few details	Few details and/or lack of focus in narrative	Not a narrative; lacks clarity and development
Organization	Uses lines and stanzas with clear sequence of events	Uses some lines and stanzas; can follow sequence	Uses lines and stanzas; one or two gaps in sequence	No lines or stanzas; sequence of events not clear	No lines, stanzas, or sequence of events
Voice	Excellent sense of writer's attitude toward topic; strongly engages audience and speaks directly to them	Clear sense of how writer feels and thinks; engages audience	Some sense of how writer feels and thinks; somewhat engages audience	Limited sense of how writer feels and thinks; weak attempt to engage audience	No sense of how writer feels and thinks about topic; no attempt to engage audience
Word Choice	Vivid style created by use of exact nouns, strong verbs, exciting adjectives, and clear figurative language	Clear style created by strong, precise words	Some style created by strong, precise words	Little style created by strong, precise words; some lack of clarity	Word choice vague or incorrect
Sentences	Clear, interesting, unique sentences	Clear sentences	Some clear sentences; some variety	Few clear sentences; no variety	Most sentences unclear; no variety of sentence structure
Conventions	Excellent control; few or no sentence errors	Good control; few sentence errors	Fair control; some errors	Weak control; some serious sentence errors	Many serious sentence errors that affect meaning

Rubric	4	3	2	1
Focus/Ideas	Vivid narration with well-chosen supporting details	Fairly vivid narrative with some details	Few details and/or lack of focus in narrative	Not a narrative; lacks clarity and development
Organization	Uses lines and stanzas with clear sequence of events	Uses some lines and stanzas; can follow sequence	No lines or stanzas; sequence of events not clear	No lines, stanzas, or sequence of events
Voice	Excellent sense of writer's attitude toward topic; strongly engages audience and speaks directly to them	Clear sense of how writer feels and thinks; engages audience	Some sense of how writer feels and thinks; weak attempt to engage audience	No sense of how writer feels and thinks about topic; no attempt to engage audience
Word Choice	Vivid style created by use of exact nouns, strong verbs, exciting adjectives, and clear figurative language	Some style created by strong, precise words	Little style created by strong, precise words; some lack of clarity	Word choice vague or incorrect
Sentences	Clear, interesting, unique sentences	Clear sentences	Some sentences clear	Most sentences unclear; no variety of sentence structure
Conventions	Excellent control; few or no sentences errors	Good control; few sentence errors	Weak control; some serious sentence errors	Many serious sentence errors that affect meaning

Rubric	6	5	4	3	2	1
Focus/Ideas	Clear moral or lesson; tells a simple story; clear use of animals as characters	Clear moral or lesson; somewhat simple story; use of animals as characters	Reasonably clear moral or lesson; somewhat simple story; some use of animals as characters	Unclear moral or lesson; story hard to follow; little use of animals as characters	No moral or lesson; story very hard to follow; little or no use of animals as characters	No attempt at a moral or lesson; can not follow story; no use of animals as characters
Organization	Organized with a clear sequence of events	Can follow sequence of events	Can reasonably follow sequence of events	Attempts to follow sequence of events	Unclear sequence of events	No sequence of events
Voice	Writer is clearly engaged with the story and its characters	Writer is interested in the story and its characters	Writer is somewhat interested in the story and its characters	Some sense of writer's interest	Weak sense of writer's interest	Writer not engaged
Word Choice	Many vivid words	Some vivid words	Few vivid words	Attempt at using vivid words	No specific details	No attempt at using vivid words
Sentences	Well-crafted sentences with strong use of statements and questions; varied sentence beginnings	Fairly well-crafted sentences with some use of statements and questions; some varied sentence beginnings	Correctly constructed sentences with some use of statements and questions; few varied sentence beginnings	Mostly corrected sentences with little use of statements and questions; little variety	Little or no use of statements and questions; no varied sentence beginnings	No use of statements and questions; incoherent sentences; no attempt at varied sentence beginnings
Conventions	Few, if any, errors in use of subject and predicate	Few minor errors in use of subject and predicate	Some minor errors in use of subject and/or predicate	Several minor errors in use of subject and/or predicate	Many errors in use of subject and/or predicate	Errors in use of subject and/or predicate detract from meaning

Rubric	5	4	3	2	1
Focus/Ideas	Clear moral or lesson; tells a simple story; clear use of animals as characters	Clear moral or lesson; somewhat simple story; use of animals as characters	Unclear moral or lesson; story hard to follow; some use of animals as characters	No moral or lesson; story very hard to follow; little or no use of animals as characters	No attempt at a moral or lesson; can not follow story; no use of animals as characters
Organization	Organized with a clear sequence of events	Can follow sequence of events	Attempts to follow sequence of events	Unclear sequence of events	No sequence of events
Voice	Writer is clearly engaged with the story and its characters	Writer is interested in the story and its characters	Some sense of writer's interest	Weak sense of writer's interest	Writer not engaged
Word Choice	Many vivid words	Some vivid words	Attempt at using vivid words	No specific details	No attempt at using vivid words
Sentences	Well-crafted sentences with strong use of statements and questions; varied sentence beginnings	Fairly well-crafted sentences with some use of statements and questions; some varied sentence beginnings	Mostly corrected sentences with little use of statements and questions; little variety	Little or no use of statements and questions; no varied sentence beginnings	No use of statements and questions; incoherent sentences; no attempt at varied sentence beginnings
Conventions	Few, if any, errors in use of subject and predicate	Few minor errors in use of subject and predicate	Several minor errors in use of subject and/or predicate	Many errors in use of subject and/or predicate	Errors in use of subject and/or predicate detract from understanding

Rubric	4	3	2	1
Focus/Ideas	Clear moral or lesson; tells a simple story; clear use of animals as characters	Unclear moral or lesson; story hard to follow; use of animals as characters	No moral or lesson; story very hard to follow; little or no use of animals as characters	No attempt at a moral or lesson; can not follow story; no use of animals as characters
Organization	Organized with a clear sequence of events	Can follow sequence of events	Unclear sequence of events	No sequence of events
Voice	Writer is clearly engaged with the story and its characters	Writer is interested in the story and its characters	Weak sense of writer's interest	Writer not engaged
Word Choice	Many vivid words	Some vivid words	No specific details	No attempt at using vivid words
Sentences	Well-crafted sentences with strong use of statements and questions; varied sentence beginnings	Fairly well-crafted sentences with some use of statements and questions; some varied sentence beginnings	Little or no use of statements and questions; no varied sentence beginnings	No use of statements and questions; incoherent sentences; no attempt at varied sentence beginnings
Conventions	Few, if any, errors in use of subject and predicate	Minor errors in use of subject and/or predicate	Many errors in use of subject and/or predicate	Errors in use of subject and/or predicate detract from understanding

Rubric	6	5	4	3	2	1
Focus/Ideas	Strong control of letter features, such as heading and closing; well-developed body	Good control of letter features, such as heading and closing; developed body	Minor errors in letter features, such as heading and closing; developed body	Some errors in letter features, such as heading and closing; somewhat developed body	Many errors in letter features, such as heading and closing; underdeveloped body	Numerous errors in letter features, such as heading and closing; undeveloped body
Organization	Clearly organized paragraphs	Organized paragraphs	Able to follow organizational pattern	Some organizational pattern	Organizational pattern attempted but not clear	No organizational pattern evident
Voice	Writer is imaginative; tone is friendly and inviting	Writer is imaginative; tone is generally friendly and inviting	Writer is generally imaginative; evidence of friendly tone	Somewhat imaginative voice and friendly tone	Attempts an imaginative voice and friendly tone	No attempt at an imaginative voice and friendly tone
Word Choice	Strong use of vivid words	Good use of vivid words	Adequate use of vivid words	Attempt at using vivid words	Weak use of vivid words	No use of vivid words
Sentences	Clear sentences of various lengths and types	Most sentences are of various lengths and types	Some sentences are of various lengths and types	Sentences of a few lengths and types	Little attempt at various lengths and types of sentences	No attempt at sentences; no attempt at various lengths and types of sentences
Conventions	Few, if any, errors; correct use of commas; sentences include statements and questions	Few minor errors; correct use of commas; most sentences include statements and questions	Some minor errors; most commas used correctly; some use of statements and questions	Several minor errors; some commas used correctly; little use of statements and questions	Many errors; inaccurate use of commas; no use of statements and questions	Numerous errors; no use of commas; no attempt at use of statements and questions

Rubric	5	4	3	2	1
Focus/Ideas	Strong control of letter features, such as heading and closing; well-developed body	Good control of letter features, such as heading and closing; developed body	Minor errors in letter features, such as heading and closing; developed body	Many errors in letter features, such as heading and closing; underdeveloped body	Numerous errors in letter features, such as heading and closing; undeveloped body
Organization	Clearly organized paragraphs	Organized paragraphs	Able to follow organizational pattern	Organizational pattern attempted but not clear	No organizational pattern evident
Voice	Writer is imaginative; tone is friendly and inviting	Writer is imaginative; tone is generally friendly and inviting	Writer is generally imaginative; evidence of friendly tone	Attempts an imaginative voice and friendly tone	No attempt at an imaginative voice and friendly tone
Word Choice	Strong use of vivid words	Good use of vivid words	Adequate use of vivid words	Weak use of vivid words	No use of vivid words
Sentences	Clear sentences of various lengths and types	Most sentences are of various lengths and types	Some sentences are of various lengths and types	Little attempt at various lengths and types of sentences	No attempt at sentences; no attempt at various lengths and types of sentences
Conventions	Few, if any, errors; correct use of commas; sentences include statements and questions	Few minor errors; correct use of commas; most sentences include statements and questions	Some minor errors; most commas used correctly; some use of statements and questions	Many errors; inaccurate use of commas; no use of statements and questions	Numerous errors; no use of commas; no attempt at use of statements and questions

Rubric	4	3	2	1
Focus/Ideas	Strong control of letter features, such as heading and closing; well-developed body	Minor errors in letter features, such as heading and closing; developed body	Many errors in letter features, such as heading and closing; underdeveloped body	Numerous errors in letter features, such as heading and closing; undeveloped body
Organization	Clearly organized paragraphs	Able to follow organizational pattern	Organizational pattern attempted but not clear	No organizational pattern evident
Voice	Writer is imaginative; tone is friendly and inviting	Some evidence of imaginative voice and friendly tone	Attempts an imaginative voice and friendly tone	No attempt at an imaginative voice and friendly tone
Word Choice	Strong use of vivid words	Adequate use of vivid words	Weak use of vivid words	No use of vivid words
Sentences	Clear sentences of various lengths and types	Sentences of a few lengths and types	Little attempt at various lengths and types of sentences	No attempt at sentences; no attempt at various lengths and types of sentences
Conventions	Few, if any, errors; correct use of commas; sentences include statements and questions	Several minor errors; mostly correct use of commas; some use of statements and questions	Many errors; inaccurate use of commas; no use of statements and questions	Numerous errors; no use of commas; no attempt at use of statements and questions

Rubric	6	5	4	3	2	1
Focus/Ideas	Clear focus and description of a person, place, or thing	Fairly clear focus and description of a person, place, or thing	Reasonably clear focus and description of a person, place, or thing	Unclear focus and description of a person, place, or thing	No focus on a person, place, or thing	No understanding of description of person, place, or thing
Organization	Clear main idea; strong use of details	Fairly clear main idea; use of details	Reasonably clear main idea; adequate use of details	Unclear main idea; adequate use of details	No main idea; unclear use of details	No attempt at a main idea; no organization of details
Voice	Writer is clearly interested in what is being described	Writer is interested in what is being described	Writer is reasonably interested in what is being described	Some evidence of interest in what is being described	Little evidence of interest in what is being described	No interest in what is being described
Word Choice	Strong use of vivid words that appeal to the senses	Use of vivid words that appeal to the senses	Some vivid words that appeal to the senses	Few vivid words that appeal to the senses	Little attempt to use vivid words; descriptions do not appeal to the senses	Incorrect or limited word choice; no detailed descriptions
Sentences	All sentences complete	Most sentences complete	Few fragments and run-on sentences	Some fragments and run-on sentences	Several fragments and run-on sentences	Little or no understanding of sentence structure
Conventions	Few, if any, errors; strong understanding of commands and exclamations	Few minor errors; understanding of commands and exclamations	Some minor errors; adequate understanding of commands and exclamations	Several minor errors; little understanding of commands and exclamations	Many errors; no understanding of commands and exclamations	Numerous errors; no attempt at commands and exclamations

Rubric	5	4	3	2	1
Focus/Ideas	Clear focus and description of a person, place, or thing	Fairly clear focus and description of a person, place, or thing	Reasonably clear focus and description of a person, place, or thing	No focus on a person, place, or thing	No understanding of description of person, place, or thing
Organization	Clear main idea; strong use of details	Fairly clear main idea; use of details	Unclear main idea; adequate use of details	No main idea; unclear use of details	No attempt at a main idea; no organization of details
Voice	Writer is clearly interested in what is being described	Writer is interested in what is being described	Some evidence of interest in what is being described	Little evidence of interest in what is being described	No interest in what is being described
Word Choice	Strong use of vivid words that appeal to the senses	Use of vivid words that appeal to the senses	Some vivid words that appeal to the senses	Little attempt to use vivid words; descriptions do not appeal to the senses	Incorrect or limited word choice; no detailed descriptions
Sentences	All sentences complete	Most sentences complete	Some fragments and run-on sentences	Several fragments and run-on sentences	Little or no understanding of sentence structure
Conventions	Few, if any, errors; strong understanding of commands and exclamations	Few minor errors; understanding of commands and exclamations	Several minor errors; adequate understanding of commands and exclamations	Many errors; no understanding of commands and exclamations	Numerous errors; no attempt at commands and exclamations

Rubric	4	3	2	1
Focus/Ideas	Clear focus and description of a person, place, or thing	Fairly clear focus and description of a person, place, or thing	No focus on a person, place, or thing	No understanding of description of person, place, or thing
Organization	Clear main idea; strong use of details	Unclear main idea; adequate use of details	No main idea; unclear use of details	No attempt at a main idea; no organization of details
Voice	Writer is clearly interested in what is being described	Some evidence of interest in what is being described	Little evidence of interest in what is being described	No interest in what is being described
Word Choice	Strong use of vivid words that appeal to the senses	Some vivid words that appeal to the senses	Little attempt to use vivid words; descriptions do not appeal to the senses	Incorrect or limited word choice; no detailed descriptions
Sentences	All sentences complete	Most sentences complete	Several fragments and run-on sentences	Little or no understanding of sentence structure
Conventions	Few, if any, errors; strong understanding of commands and exclamations	Several minor errors; adequate understanding of commands and exclamations	Many errors; no understanding of commands and exclamations	Numerous errors; no attempt at commands and exclamations

Rubric	6	5	4	3	2	1
Focus/Ideas	Vivid narrative; well-developed characters and setting; realistic	Clear narrative; developed characters and setting; realistic	Good narrative; adequate characterization and setting	Narrative has unclear focus on characters and setting; somewhat realistic	Narrative lacking focus on characters or setting; somewhat unrealistic	Narrative with no focus on characters or setting; unrealistic
Organization	Clear series of events	Fairly clear series of events	Able to follow series of events	Attempt at series of events	Unclear series of events	No series of events
Voice	Voice always matches word choice	Voice mostly matches word choice	Voice reasonably matches word choice	Voice sometimes matches word choice	Voice rarely matches word choice	Voice never matches word choice
Word Choice	Strong use of precise words	Use of precise words	Reasonable use of precise words	Little use of precise words	Weak use of precise words	No use of precise words
Sentences	Clear sentences of various lengths and types	Fairly clear sentences of various lengths and types	Few sentences of various lengths and types	Sentences of a few lengths and types	Sentences of similar length and type	No attempt at sentences of various lengths and types
Conventions	Few, if any, errors; correct use of compound sentences	Few minor errors; correct use of compound sentences	Several small errors; mostly correct use of compound sentences	Many errors; some correct use of compound sentences	Many errors; weak use of compound sentences	Many serious errors; incorrect or no use of compound sentences

Rubric	5	4	3	2	1
Focus/Ideas	Vivid narrative; well-developed characters and setting; realistic	Clear narrative; developed characters and setting; realistic	Good narrative; adequate characterization and setting	Narrative lacking focus on characters or setting; somewhat unrealistic	Narrative with no focus on characters or setting; unrealistic
Organization	Clear series of events	Fairly clear series of events	Able to follow series of events	Unclear series of events	No series of events
Voice	Voice always matches word choice	Voice mostly matches word choice	Voice sometimes matches word choice	Voice rarely matches word choice	Voice never matches word choice
Word Choice	Strong use of precise words	Use of precise words	Some use of precise words	Weak use of precise words	No use of precise words
Sentences	Clear sentences of various lengths and types	Fairly clear sentences of various lengths and types	Sentences of a few lengths and types	Sentences of similar length and type	No attempt at sentences of various lengths and types
Conventions	Few, if any, errors; correct use of compound sentences	Few minor errors; correct use of compound sentences	Several small errors; mostly correct use of compound sentences	Many errors; weak use of compound sentences	Many serious errors; incorrect or no use of compound sentences

Rubric	4	3	2	1
Focus/Ideas	Vivid narrative; well-developed characters and setting; realistic	Good narrative; adequate characterization and setting	Narrative lacking focus on characters or setting; somewhat unrealistic	Narrative with no focus on characters or setting; unrealistic
Organization	Clear series of events	Able to follow series of events	Unclear series of events	No series of events
Voice	Voice always matches word choice	Voice mostly matches word choice	Voice rarely matches word choice	Voice never matches word choice
Word Choice	Strong use of precise words	Some use of precise words	Weak use of precise words	No use of precise words
Sentences	Clear sentences of various lengths and types	Sentences of a few lengths and types	Sentences of similar length and type	No attempt at sentences of various lengths and types
Conventions	Few, if any, errors; correct use of compound sentences	Several small errors; correct use of compound sentences	Many errors; weak use of compound sentences	Many serious errors; incorrect or no use of compound sentences

Rubric	6	5	4	3	2	1
Focus/Ideas	Exciting story with interesting characters; amazing or heroic events	Good story with developed characters; amazing or heroic events	Reasonably good story with developed characters; somewhat amazing or heroic events	Story has some focus on characters; somewhat amazing events	Story has little focus on characters; events are not very amazing or heroic	Story has no focus on characters; events are not amazing or heroic
Organization	Clear order of events	Can follow order of events	Reasonable organization of order of events	Order of events fairly unclear	Unclear order of events	No order of events
Voice	Writer shows high interest in the story and the characters	Writer shows interest in the story and the characters	Writer shows some interest in the story and the characters	Writer shows little interest in the story and the characters	Writer is not interested in the story or characters	Writer makes no effort to show interest in the story or characters
Word Choice	Strong use of vivid verbs to bring the story to life	Good use of vivid verbs to bring the story to life	Good try at using vivid verbs	Little use of vivid verbs; story is somewhat dull	Poor use of vivid verbs; story is dull	No effort made to use vivid verbs
Sentences	Clear sentences of different lengths and types	Most sentences are of various lengths and types	Some sentences are of various lengths and types	Sentences of a few lengths and types	Sentences of similar length and type	No variety of sentence length and type
Conventions	Few, if any, errors; correct use of singular and plural nouns	Few minor errors; mostly correct use of singular and plural nouns	Some small errors; use of singular and plural nouns	Several small errors; use of singular and plural nouns	Many errors; weak use of singular and plural nouns	Many serious errors; incorrect or no use of singular and plural nouns

Rubric	5	4	3	2	1
Focus/Ideas	Exciting story with interesting characters; amazing or heroic events	Good story with developed characters; amazing or heroic events	Reasonably good story with developed characters; somewhat amazing or heroic events	Story has little focus on characters; events are not very amazing or heroic	Story has no focus on characters; events are not amazing or heroic
Organization	Clear order of events	Can follow order of events	Reasonable organization of order of events	Unclear order of events	No order of events
Voice	Writer shows high interest in the story and the characters	Writer shows interest in the story and the characters	Writer shows some interest in the story and the characters	Writer is not interested in the story or characters	Writer makes no effort to show interest in the story or characters
Word Choice	Strong use of vivid verbs to bring the story to life	Good use of vivid verbs to bring the story to life	Good try at using vivid verbs	Poor use of vivid verbs; story is dull	No effort made to use vivid verbs
Sentences	Clear sentences of different lengths and types	Most sentences are of various lengths and types	Some sentences are of various lengths and types	Sentences of similar length and type	No variety of sentence length and type
Conventions	Few, if any, errors; correct use of singular and plural nouns	Few minor errors; mostly correct use of singular and plural nouns	Some small errors; use of singular and plural nouns	Many errors; weak use of singular and plural nouns	Many serious errors; incorrect or no use of singular and plural nouns

Rubric	4	3	2	1
Focus/Ideas	Exciting story with interesting characters; amazing or heroic events	Good story with developed characters; somewhat amazing or heroic events	Story has some focus on characters; events are not very amazing or heroic	Story has no focus on characters; events are not amazing or heroic
Organization	Clear order of events	Can follow order of events	Unclear order of events	No order of events
Voice	Writer shows interest in the story and the characters	Writer shows some interest in the story and the characters	Writer is not interested in the story or characters	Writer makes no effort to show interest in the story or characters
Word Choice	Strong use of vivid verbs to bring the story to life	Good try at using vivid verbs	Poor use of vivid verbs; story is dull	No effort made to use vivid verbs
Sentences	Clear sentences of different lengths and types	Sentences of a few lengths and types	Sentences of similar length and type	No variety of sentence length and type
Conventions	Few, if any, errors; correct use of singular and plural nouns	Several small errors; use of singular and plural nouns	Many errors; weak use of singular and plural nouns	Many serious errors; incorrect or no use of singular and plural nouns

ADVERTISEMENT

Rubric	6	5	4	3	2	1
Focus/Ideas	Focused ideas about the topic with many supporting details	Most ideas about the topic are focused and supported by details	Ideas about the topic are reasonably focused and somewhat supported by details	Some ideas and details are unclear	Some ideas are unclear and do not add to the focus of the advertisement	Advertisement is unfocused and difficult to understand
Organization	Organized logically with a strong beginning and ending	Mostly solid organization and fairly strong beginning and ending	Reasonable organization and adequate beginning and ending	Organization is unclear	Organization is unclear and beginning and/or ending is weak	Writing is unorganized and features a weak beginning and ending
Voice	Writing is engaging and shows the writer's feelings about the topic	Most of the writing has a strong voice and connects with the reader	Writing has a reasonable voice and somewhat connects with the reader	Voice occasionally weak and in many places does not show the writer's feelings	Voice is weak and does not show the writer's feelings	Writing is dull and does not reveal the voice of the writer
Word Choice	Writing includes vivid, precise words	Writing includes many strong word choices	Writing includes adequate word choices	Writing includes some vivid and interesting words	Does not include enough vivid and interesting words to express ideas	Incorrect word choices and no vivid words
Sentences	Correct and varied sentences	Fairly correct and varied sentences	Most sentences correct; some variety	Some sentences incorrect; some variety	Some sentences incorrect; little variety	Incorrect sentences; no variety
Conventions	Strong control of language; accurate use of plural nouns	Few errors and most plural nouns are used correctly	Contains few grammatical errors, including plural noun errors	Contains some grammatical errors, including plural noun errors	Contains many grammatical errors, including plural noun errors	Writing has numerous grammatical errors; meaning is lost

Rubric	5	4	3	2	1
Focus/Ideas	Focused ideas about the topic with many supporting details	Most ideas about the topic are focused and supported by details	Ideas about the topic are reasonably focused and somewhat supported by details	Some ideas are unclear and do not add to the focus of the advertisement	Advertisement is unfocused and difficult to understand
Organization	Organized logically with a strong beginning and ending	Mostly solid organization and fairly strong beginning and ending	Reasonable organization and adequate beginning and ending	Organization is unclear and beginning and/or ending is weak	Writing is unorganized and features a weak beginning and ending
Voice	Writing is engaging and shows the writer's feelings about the topic	Most of the writing has a strong voice and connects with the reader	Writing has a reasonable voice and somewhat connects with the reader	Voice is weak and in many places does not show the writer's feelings	Writing is dull and does not reveal the voice of the writer
Word Choice	Writing includes vivid, precise words	Writing includes many strong word choices	Writing includes adequate word choices	Does not include enough vivid and interesting words to express ideas	Incorrect word choices and no vivid words
Sentences	Correct and varied sentences	Fairly correct and varied sentences	Most sentences correct; some variety	Some sentences incorrect; little variety	Incorrect sentences; no variety
Conventions	Strong control of language; accurate use of plural nouns	Few errors and most plural nouns are used correctly	Contains few grammatical errors, including plural noun errors	Contains some grammatical errors, including plural noun errors	Writing has many grammatical errors; meaning is lost

Rubric	4	3	2	1
Focus/Ideas	Focused ideas about the topic with many supporting details	Most ideas about the topic are focused and supported by details	Some ideas are unclear and do not add to the focus of the advertisement	Advertisement is unfocused and difficult to understand
Organization	Organized logically with a strong beginning and ending	Mostly solid organization and fairly strong beginning and ending	Organization is unclear and beginning and/or ending is weak	Writing is unorganized and features a weak beginning and ending
Voice	Writing is engaging and shows the writer's feelings about the topic	Most of the writing has a strong voice and connects with the reader	Voice is weak and in many places does not show the writer's feelings	Writing is dull and does not reveal the voice of the writer
Word Choice	Writing includes vivid, precise words	Writing includes many strong word choices	Does not include enough vivid and interesting words to express ideas	Incorrect word choices and no vivid words
Sentences	Correct and varied sentences	Most sentences correct; some variety	Some sentences incorrect; little variety	Incorrect sentences; no variety
Conventions	Strong control of language; accurate use of plural nouns	Few errors and most plural nouns are used correctly	Contains some grammatical errors, including plural noun errors	Writing has many grammatical errors; meaning is lost

Rubric	6	5	4	3	2	1
Focus/Ideas	Clear, well-developed letter; the ideas and purpose of the letter are clear.	Good letter; the ideas and purpose are fairly clear	Fairly good letter; the ideas and purpose are adequate	The ideas and purpose are somewhat weak and not well-developed	The ideas and purpose are weak and underdeveloped	The ideas lack clarity. The letter lacks purpose.
Organization	Ideas are organized logically; no gaps	Ideas are organized logically; one or two gaps	Ideas are organized logically; few gaps	Some organizational pattern	Organizational pattern attempted but not clear	No organizational pattern evident
Voice	Friendly and engaging tone	Mostly friendly tone	Generally friendly tone	Somewhat friendly tone	Attempts a friendly tone	Unfriendly tone
Word Choice	Vivid, precise word choice	Accurate word choice	Adequate word choice	Limited word choice	Weak or repetitive word choice	Incorrect or very limited word choice
Sentences	All sentences complete	Most sentences complete	Few sentence fragments or run-on sentences	Some sentence fragments or run-on sentences	Mostly sentence fragments or run-on sentences	Little or no understanding of sentence structure
Conventions	Few, if any, errors; correct use of singular possessive nouns	Few minor errors; mostly correct use of singular possessive nouns	Some minor errors; mostly correct use of singular possessive nouns	Several minor errors; weak use of singular possessive nouns	Many errors; weak use of possessive nouns	Numerous errors; no or incorrect use of possessive nouns

Rubric	5	4	3	2	1
Focus/Ideas	Clear, well-developed letter; the ideas and purpose of the letter are clear.	Good letter; the ideas and purpose are fairly clear	Fairly good letter; the ideas and purpose are adequate	The ideas and purpose are weak and not well-developed	The ideas lack clarity. The letter lacks purpose.
Organization	Ideas are organized logically; no gaps	Ideas are organized logically; one or two gaps	Ideas are organized logically; few gaps	Organizational pattern attempted but not clear	No organizational pattern evident
Voice	Friendly and engaging tone	Mostly friendly tone	Generally friendly tone	Somewhat friendly tone	Unfriendly tone
Word Choice	Vivid, precise word choice	Accurate word choice	Adequate word choice	Limited or repetitive word choice	Incorrect or very limited word choice
Sentences	All sentences complete	Most sentences complete	Few sentence fragments or run-on sentences	Some sentence fragments or run-on sentences	Little or no understanding of sentence structure
Conventions	Few, if any, errors; correct use of singular possessive nouns	Few minor errors; mostly correct use of singular possessive nouns	Some minor errors; mostly correct use of singular possessive nouns	Many errors; weak use of possessive nouns	Numerous errors; no or incorrect use of possessive nouns

Rubric	4	3	2	1
Focus/Ideas	Clear, well-developed letter; the ideas and purpose of the letter are clear.	Good letter; the ideas and purpose are adequate.	The ideas and purpose are weak and not well-developed	The ideas lack clarity. The letter lacks purpose.
Organization	Ideas are organized logically; no gaps	Ideas are organized logically; few gaps	Organizational pattern attempted but not clear	No organizational pattern evident
Voice	Friendly and engaging tone	Mostly friendly tone	Somewhat friendly tone	Unfriendly tone
Word Choice	Vivid, precise word choice	Accurate word choice	Limited or repetitive word choice	Incorrect or very limited word choice
Sentences	All sentences complete	Most sentences complete	Some sentence fragments or run-on sentences	Little or no understanding of sentence structure
Conventions	Few, if any, errors; correct use of singular possessive nouns	Several minor errors; mostly correct use of singular possessive nouns	Many errors; weak use of possessive nouns	Numerous errors; no or incorrect use of possessive nouns

Rubric	6	5	4	3	2	1
Focus/Ideas	Directions are well focused and fully developed	Directions are focused and mostly developed	Directions are reasonably focused and developed	Directions not clearly focused and underdeveloped	Directions stray from the subject or lack necessary details	Directions lack focus or have insufficient information
Organization	Organized logically into paragraphs; follows a clear sequence of instructions	Organized logically into paragraphs for the most part; sequence is clear	Organized reasonably into paragraphs; sequence is clear with minor gaps	Somewhat organized into paragraphs; several gaps in sequence	Organizational pattern is attempted but is not clear; weak sequence of instructions	No organizational pattern evident; instructions presented in random order
Voice	Instructions are thorough and clear throughout	Instructions are thorough and clear with a couple of lapses	Instructions are adequately thorough and clear with few lapses	Instructions are somewhat vague	Instructions are mostly vague with some attempt at clarity	Instructions are too unclear to be followed
Word Choice	Vivid, descriptive words; good use of time-order words	Several vivid words; use of time-order words	Reasonable amount of vivid words; some use of time-order words	Some vivid words; few time-order words	Few vivid words; few or no time-order words	Incorrect or limited word choice
Sentences	Clear sentences; good use of commands	Mostly clear sentences; several commands	Some clear sentences; some commands	Little variety; few commands	Little or no variety; no commands	Incorrect sentences; no commands
Conventions	Few, if any, errors; plural possessive nouns used correctly	Few errors; plural possessive nouns generally used correctly	Some errors; plural possessive nouns sometimes used correctly	Few errors that may interfere with understanding; plural possessive nouns rarely used correctly	Some errors that may interfere with understanding; plural possessive nouns used incorrectly	Serious errors that may prevent understanding; plural possessive nouns used incorrectly

Rubric	5	4	3	2	1
Focus/Ideas	Directions are well focused and fully developed	Directions are focused and mostly developed	Directions are generally focused and developed	Directions stray from the subject or lack necessary details	Directions lack focus or have insufficient information
Organization	Organized logically into paragraphs; follows a clear sequence of instructions	Organized logically into paragraphs for the most part; sequence is clear	Organized reasonably into paragraphs; sequence is clear with minor gaps	Organizational pattern is attempted but is not clear; weak sequence of instructions	No organizational pattern evident; instructions presented in random order
Voice	Instructions are thorough and clear throughout	Instructions are thorough and clear with a couple of lapses	Instructions are adequately thorough and clear with few lapses	Instructions are mostly vague with an attempt at clarity	Instructions are too unclear to be followed
Word Choice	Vivid, descriptive words; good use of time-order words	Several vivid words; use of time-order words	Reasonable amount of vivid words; some use of time-order words	Few vivid words; few or no time-order words	Incorrect or limited word choice
Sentences	Clear sentences; good use of commands	Mostly clear sentences; several commands	Some clear sentences; some commands	Little or no variety; no commands	Incorrect sentences; no commands
Conventions	Few, if any, errors; plural possessive nouns used correctly	Few errors; plural possessive nouns generally used correctly	Some errors; plural possessive nouns sometimes used correctly	Some errors that may interfere with understanding; plural possessive nouns used incorrectly	Serious errors that may prevent understanding; plural possessive nouns used incorrectly

Rubric	4	3	2	1
Focus/Ideas	Directions are well focused and fully developed	Directions generally focused and developed	Directions stray from the subject or lack necessary details	Directions lack focus or have insufficient information
Organization	Organized logically into paragraphs; follows a clear sequence of instructions	Organized logically into paragraphs for the most part; sequence is clear with minor gaps	Organizational pattern is attempted but is not clear; weak sequence of instructions	No organizational pattern evident; instructions presented in random order
Voice	Instructions are thorough and clear throughout	Instructions are thorough and clear with some lapses	Instructions are mostly vague with an attempt at clarity	Instructions are too unclear to be followed
Word Choice	Vivid, descriptive words; good use of time-order words	Some vivid words; some use of time-order words	Few vivid words; few or no time-order words	Incorrect or limited word choice
Sentences	Clear sentences; use of commands	Mostly clear sentences; some commands	Little or no variety; no commands	Incorrect sentences; no commands
Conventions	Few, if any, errors; plural possessive nouns used correctly	Few errors; plural possessive nouns generally used correctly	Some errors that may interfere with understanding; plural possessive nouns used incorrectly	Serious errors that may prevent understanding; plural possessive nouns used incorrectly

Rubric	6	5	4	3	2	1
Focus/Ideas	Vivid narrative with well-developed characters and setting	Narrative with good characterization and setting; good details	Narrative with adequate characterization and setting; some details	Narrative has some focus; few details	Narrative lacking focus; no details	Not a narrative; no focus on characters or setting
Organization	Clear sequence of events	Can follow sequence of events	Reasonable organization of sequence of events	Sequence of events somewhat unclear	Unclear sequence of events	No sequence of events
Voice	Clear sense of writer's personality	Writer engaged with subject	Writer sometimes engaged with subject	Writer shows little interest with subject	Weak voice	No voice; writer not engaged
Word Choice	Strong use of specific details to elaborate	Good use of specific details	Some specific details	Tells in general terms; few specific details	Tells in general terms; no specific details	No attempt at elaboration; no specific details
Sentences	Clear sentences of various lengths and types; strong variety of sentences beginning; strong focus on main idea	Most sentences are of various lengths and types; variety of sentence beginnings; good focus on main idea	Some sentences are of various lengths and types; some variety of sentence beginnings; focus on main idea	Sentences of a few lengths and types; little variety of sentence beginnings; some focus on main idea	Sentences of similar length and type; weak variety of sentence beginnings; little to no focus on main idea	No attempt at sentences of various lengths and types; no variety of sentence beginnings; no focus on main idea
Conventions	Few, if any, errors; strong use of action and linking verbs	Few minor errors; good use of action and linking verbs	Some minor errors; use of action and linking verbs	Several minor errors; little use of action and linking verbs	Many errors; weak use of action and linking verbs	Numerous errors; no use of action and linking verbs

Rubric	5	4	3	2	1
Focus/Ideas	Vivid narrative with well-developed characters and setting	Narrative with good characterization and setting; good details	Narrative with adequate characterization and setting; some details	Narrative lacking focus; no details	Not a narrative; no focus on characters or setting
Organization	Clear sequence of events	Can follow sequence of events	Reasonable organization of sequence of events	Unclear sequence of events	No sequence of events
Voice	Clear sense of writer's personality	Writer engaged with subject	Writer sometimes engaged with subject	Weak voice	No voice; writer not engaged
Word Choice	Strong use of specific details to elaborate	Good use of specific details	Some specific details	Tells in general terms; no specific details	No attempt at elaboration; no specific details
Sentences	Clear sentences of various lengths and types; strong variety of sentence beginning; strong focus on main idea	Most sentences are of various lengths and types; variety of sentence beginnings; good focus on main idea	Some sentences are of various lengths and types; some variety of sentence beginnings; focus on main idea	Sentences of similar length and type; weak variety of sentence beginnings; little to no focus on main idea	No attempt at sentences of various lengths and types; no variety of sentence beginnings; no focus on main idea
Conventions	Few, if any, errors; strong use of action and linking verbs	Few minor errors; good use of action and linking verbs	Some minor errors; use of action and linking verbs	Many errors; weak use of action and linking verbs	Numerous errors; no use of action and linking verbs

Rubric	4	3	2	1
Focus/Ideas	Vivid narrative with well-developed characters and setting	Narrative with good characterization and setting; some details	Narrative lacking focus; few details	Not a narrative; no focus on characters or setting
Organization	Clear sequence of events	Can follow sequence of events	Unclear sequence of events	No sequence of events
Voice	Clear sense of writer's personality	Writer engaged with subject	Weak voice	No voice; writer not engaged
Word Choice	Strong use of specific details to elaborate	Some specific details	Tells in general terms; no specific details	No attempt at elaboration; no specific details
Sentences	Clear sentences of various lengths and types; strong variety of sentences beginning; focus on main idea	Sentences of a few lengths and types; variety of sentence beginnings; some focus on main idea	Sentences of similar length and type; weak variety of sentence beginnings; little to no focus on main idea	No attempt at sentences of various lengths and types; no variety of sentence beginnings; no focus on main idea
Conventions	Few, if any, errors; strong use of action and linking verbs	Several minor errors; use of action and linking verbs	Many errors; weak use of action and linking verbs	Numerous errors; no use of action and linking verbs

Rubric	6	5	4	3	2	1
Focus/Ideas	Has clear plot focus; well-developed setting and characters; clear resolution	Has plot and good focus; developed characters and setting; developed resolution	Has adequate plot and focus; has characters and a setting; has resolution	Has some plot and focus; underdeveloped setting, characters, and resolution	Lacks plot and focus; poorly developed setting and characters; little or no resolution	No plot; no focus; lacks plausible setting and characters; no resolution
Organization	Correct use of play format	Use of play format	Adequate use of play format	Attempt to use play format	Incorrect use of play format	No attempt at using play format
Voice	Consistent voice appropriate to theme and purpose	Voice mostly consistent and appropriate to theme and purpose	Voice adequately consistent and appropriate to theme and purpose	Voice sometimes inconsistent and/or inappropriate to theme and purpose	Inconsistent voice or voice inappropriate to theme and purpose	No attempt to create voice
Word Choice	Clear, concise character dialogue; reveals character traits; describes action	Clear dialogue; reveals most character traits; describes most action	Somewhat clear dialogue; reveals some character traits; describes some action	Attempt to create dialogue; reveals little character; describes little action	Flat, unclear dialogue; does not reveal character; does not describe action	No attempt to create coherent dialogue
Sentences	Clear sentences of various lengths and types	Most sentences are of various lengths and types	Some sentences are of various lengths and types	Sentences of a few lengths and types	Sentences of similar length and type	No attempt at sentences of various lengths and types
Conventions	Few, if any, errors; strong use of main and helping verbs; correct punctuation	Few minor errors; correct use of main and helping verbs; mostly correct punctuation	Some minor errors; some use of main and helping verbs; some correct punctuation	Several minor errors; attempt to use main and helping verbs; mostly incorrect punctuation	Many errors; weak use of main and helping verbs; incorrect punctuation	Numerous errors; no use of main or helping verbs; no or incorrect punctuation

Rubric	5	4	3	2	1
Focus/Ideas	Has clear plot focus; well-developed setting and characters; clear resolution	Has plot and good focus; developed characters and setting; developed resolution	Has adequate plot and focus; has a setting and characters; has resolution	Lacks plot and focus; poorly developed setting and characters; little or no resolution	No plot; no focus; lacks plausible setting and characters; no resolution
Organization	Correct use of play format	Use of play format	Adequate use of play format	Incorrect use of play format	No attempt at using play format
Voice	Consistent voice appropriate to theme and purpose	Voice mostly consistent and appropriate to theme and purpose	Voice adequately consistent and appropriate to theme and purpose	Inconsistent voice or voice inappropriate to theme and purpose	No attempt to create voice
Word Choice	Clear, concise character dialogue; reveals character traits; describes action	Fairly clear dialogue; reveals most character traits; describes most action	Somewhat clear dialogue; reveals some character traits; describes some action	Flat, unclear dialogue; does not reveal character; does not describe action	No attempt to create coherent dialogue
Sentences	Clear sentences of various lengths and types	Most sentences are of various lengths and types	Some sentences are of various lengths and types	Sentences of similar length and type	No attempt at sentences of various lengths and types
Conventions	Few, if any, errors; strong use of main and helping verbs; correct punctuation	Few minor errors; correct use of main and helping verbs; mostly correct punctuation	Some minor errors; some use of main and helping verbs; some correct punctuation	Many errors; weak use of main and helping verbs; incorrect punctuation	Numerous errors; no use of main or helping verbs; no or incorrect punctuation

Rubric	4	3	2	1
Focus/Ideas	Has clear plot focus; well-developed setting and characters; clear resolution	Has plot and some focus; has a setting and characters; has resolution	Lacks plot and focus; poorly developed setting and characters; little or no resolution	No plot; no focus; lacks plausible setting and characters; no resolution
Organization	Correct use of play format	Use of play format	Incorrect use of play format	No attempt at using play format
Voice	Consistent voice appropriate to theme and purpose	Voice somewhat consistent and appropriate to theme and purpose	Inconsistent or inappropriate voice for theme and purpose	No attempt to create voice
Word Choice	Clear, concise character dialogue; reveals character traits; describes action	Somewhat clear dialogue; reveals some character traits; describes some action	Flat, unclear dialogue; does not reveal character; does not describe action	No attempt to create coherent dialogue
Sentences	Clear sentences of various lengths and types	Sentences of a few lengths and types	Sentences of similar length and type	No attempt at sentences of various lengths and types
Conventions	Few, if any, errors; strong use of main and helping verbs; correct punctuation	Several minor errors; use of main and helping verbs; mostly correct punctuation	Many errors; weak use of main and helping verbs; incorrect punctuation	Numerous errors; no use of main or helping verbs; no or incorrect punctuation

Rubric	6	5	4	3	2	1
Focus/Ideas	Clear purpose and ideas; strong focus on request	Fairly clear purpose and ideas; fairly strong focus on request	Adequate description of purpose and ideas; adequate focus on request	Somewhat unclear purpose and idea; some focus on request	Unclear purpose and ideas; little focus on request	No purpose; no focus on request
Organization	Appropriate formal letter format	Mostly appropriate format chosen	Reasonable format chosen	Attempt at formal letter format	Incorrect format	No attempt at a formal letter format
Voice	Strong, polite voice; writer's personality conveyed	Mostly strong voice; shows writer's personality	Reasonably strong voice; polite voice	Somewhat weak voice; attempt at polite voice	Weak or impolite voice	No voice; writer not engaged
Word Choice	Strong use of precise and appropriate words	Accurate use of precise and appropriate words	Use of some precise and appropriate words	Limited word choice	Lacks precise or appropriate words	No attempt at using precise or appropriate words
Sentences	Good mix of sentence lengths, kinds	Most sentences are of various lengths and kinds	Some variety in sentence lengths, kinds	Little variety in sentence lengths, kinds	Many sentences lacking fluency and variety	Sentences choppy and dull
Conventions	Correct use of comma, closing, and full signature; few, if any, errors; strong understanding of subject-verb agreement	Mostly correct use of comma, closing, and full signature; few minor errors; understanding of subject-verb agreement	Some correct use of commas, closing, and signature; some minor errors; adequate understanding of subject-verb agreement	Incorrect use of commas, closing, or signature; several minor errors; weak understanding of subject-verb agreement	Incorrect use of comma, closing, and signature; many errors; no understanding of subject-verb agreement	Closing and signature are missing; numerous errors; no attempt at subject-verb agreement

Rubric	5	4	3	2	1
Focus/Ideas	Clear purpose and ideas; strong focus on request	Fairly clear purpose and ideas; fairly strong focus on request	Adequate description of purpose and ideas; adequate focus on request	Unclear purpose and ideas; little focus on request	No purpose; no focus on request
Organization	Appropriate formal letter format	Mostly appropriate format chosen	Reasonable format chosen	Incorrect format	No attempt at a formal letter format
Voice	Strong, polite voice; writer's personality conveyed	Mostly strong voice; shows writer's personality	Reasonably strong voice; polite voice	Weak or impolite voice	No voice; writer not engaged
Word Choice	Strong use of precise and appropriate words	Accurate use of precise and appropriate words	Use of some precise and appropriate words	Lacks precise or appropriate words	No attempt at using precise or appropriate words
Sentences	Good mix of sentence lengths, kinds	Most sentences are of various lengths and kinds	Some variety in sentence lengths, kinds	Many sentences lacking fluency and variety	Sentences choppy and dull
Conventions	Correct use of comma, closing, and full signature; few, if any, errors; strong understanding of subject-verb agreement	Mostly correct use of comma, closing, and full signature; few minor errors; understanding of subject-verb agreement	Some correct use of commas, closing, and signature; some minor errors; adequate understanding of subject-verb agreement	Incorrect use of comma, closing, and signature; many errors; no understanding of subject-verb agreement	Closing and signature are missing; numerous errors; no attempt at subject-verb agreement

Rubric	4	3	2	1
Focus/Ideas	Clear purpose and ideas; strong focus on request	Adequate description of purpose and ideas; adequate focus on request	Unclear purpose and ideas; little focus on request	No purpose; no focus on request
Organization	Appropriate formal letter format	Reasonable format chosen	Incorrect format	No attempt at a formal letter format
Voice	Strong, polite voice; writer's personality conveyed	Reasonably strong voice; polite voice	Weak or impolite voice	No voice; writer not engaged
Word Choice	Strong use of precise and appropriate words	Use of some precise and appropriate words	Lacks precise or appropriate words	No attempt at using precise or appropriate words
Sentences	Good mix of sentence lengths, kinds	Some variety in sentence lengths, kinds	Many sentences lacking fluency and variety	Sentences choppy and dull
Conventions	Correct use of comma, closing, and full signature; few, if any, errors; strong understanding of subject-verb agreement	Mostly correct use of commas, closing, and signature; several minor errors; adequate understanding of subject-verb agreement	Incorrect use of comma, closing, and signature; many errors; no understanding of subject-verb agreement	Closing and signature are missing; numerous errors; no attempt at subject-verb agreement

Rubric	6	5	4	3	2	1
Focus/Ideas	Tight focus on topic details; strong use of headlines and subheadings	Clear focus on topic details; use of headlines and subheadings	Fairly clear focus on topic details; adequate use of headlines and subheadings	Somewhat unclear focus on topic details; some use of headlines and subheadings	No focus on topic details; weak use of headlines and subheadings	Unclear topic; no focus; no use of headlines and subheadings
Organization	Well-developed main idea; strong supporting details	Clear main idea; supporting details	Somewhat clear main idea; some supporting details	Somewhat unclear main idea; some supporting details	Unclear main idea; few supporting details	No main idea; no supporting details
Voice	Writer is clearly interested in the topic; strong use of lively details	Writer is mostly interested in the topic; use of lively details	Some evidence of writer's interest in the topic; some lively details	Interest in topic somewhat unclear; few lively details	Unclear interest in topic; no lively details	No interest in the topic; no details
Word Choice	Strong use of precise details; strong visualization	Good use of precise details; clear visualization	Good attempt at using precise words; some visualization	Few precise words; little visualization	Poor use of precise words; no visualization	No attempt at using precise words; no visualization
Sentences	Clear sentences of various lengths and types; strong variety of sentence beginnings	Mostly clear sentences of various lengths and types; good variety of sentence beginnings	Some clear sentences of various lengths and types; some variety of sentence beginnings	Sentences of a few lengths and types; little variety of sentence beginnings	Sentences of similar length and type; weak variety of sentence beginnings	No sentences; no variety of sentence beginnings
Conventions	Few, if any, errors; strong use of verb tense	Few minor errors; good use of verb tense	Some minor errors; correct use of verb tense	Several minor errors; attempt to use verb tense	Many errors; weak use of verb tenses	Numerous errors; incorrect use of verb tenses

Rubric	5	4	3	2	1
Focus/Ideas	Tight focus on topic details; strong use of headlines and subheadings	Clear focus on topic details; use of headlines and subheadings	Fairly clear focus on topic details; adequate use of headlines and subheadings	No focus on topic details; weak use of headlines and subheadings	Unclear topic; no focus; no use of headlines and subheadings
Organization	Well-developed main idea; strong supporting details	Clear main idea; supporting details	Somewhat clear main idea; some supporting details	Unclear main idea; few supporting details	No main idea; no supporting details
Voice	Writer is clearly interested in the topic; strong use of lively details	Writer is mostly interested in the topic; use of lively details	Some evidence of writer's interest in the topic; some lively details	Unclear interest in topic; no lively details	No interest in the topic; no details
Word Choice	Strong use of precise details; strong visualization	Good use of precise details; clear visualization	Good attempt at using precise words; some visualization	Poor use of precise words; no visualization	No attempt at using precise words; no visualization
Sentences	Clear sentences of various lengths and types; strong variety of sentence beginnings	Mostly clear sentences of various lengths and types; good variety of sentence beginnings	Some clear sentences of various lengths and types; some variety of sentence beginnings	Sentences of similar length and type; weak variety of sentence beginnings	No sentences; no variety of sentence beginnings
Conventions	Few, if any, errors; strong use of verb tense	Few minor errors; good use of verb tense	Some minor errors; correct use of verb tense	Many errors; weak use of verb tenses	Numerous errors; incorrect use of verb tenses

Rubric	4	3	2	1
Focus/Ideas	Tight focus on topic details; strong use of headlines and subheadings	Fairly clear focus on topic details; some use of headlines and subheadings	No focus on topic details; weak use of headlines and subheadings	Unclear topic; no focus; no use of headlines and subheadings
Organization	Well-developed main idea; strong supporting details	Clear main idea; supporting details	Unclear main idea; few supporting details	No main idea; no supporting details
Voice	Writer is clearly interested in the topic; strong use of lively details	Some evidence of writer's interest in the topic; some lively details	Unclear interest in topic; no lively details	No interest in the topic; no details
Word Choice	Strong use of precise details; strong visualization	Good attempt at using precise words; some visualization	Poor use of precise words; no visualization	No attempt at using precise words; no visualization
Sentences	Clear sentences of various lengths and types; strong variety of sentence beginnings	Sentences of a few lengths and types; good variety of sentence beginnings	Sentences of similar length and type; weak variety of sentence beginnings	No sentences; no variety of sentence beginnings
Conventions	Few, if any, errors; strong use of verb tense	Several minor errors; good use of verb tense	Many errors; weak use of verb tenses	Numerous errors; incorrect use of verb tenses

COMPARE AND CONTRAST ESSAY

Rubric	6	5	4	3	2	1
Focus/Ideas	Strong composition; compares and contrasts effectively	Good composition; compares and contrasts	Reasonably good composition; compares and contrasts adequately	Somewhat good composition; somewhat compares and contrasts	Weak composition; poorly compares and/or contrasts	Poor composition; neither compares nor contrasts
Organization	Similarities and differences in clear order; includes strong concluding statement	Similarities and differences in fairly clear order; includes well-developed conclusion	Similarities and differences in adequately clear order; includes adequate conclusion	Similarities and differences in confused order; includes slightly weak conclusion	Similarities and differences in confused order; vague or weak conclusion	No similarities and differences; no conclusion
Voice	Writer shows high interest in the subject	Writer shows interest in the subject	Writer shows some interest in the subject	Writer shows little interest in the subject	Writer shows very little interest in the subject	Writer shows no interest in the subject
Word Choice	Strong use of compare/contrast words	Good use of compare/contrast words	Adequate use of compare/contrast words	Some use of compare/contrast words	Weak use of compare/contrast words	Poor or no use of compare/contrast words
Sentences	Sentences with different lengths and beginnings	Most sentences are of various lengths and beginnings	Some sentences are of various lengths and beginnings	Sentences with a few different lengths and beginnings	Sentences with similar lengths and beginnings	No variety in sentence lengths and beginnings
Conventions	Few or no errors; strong use of irregular verbs	Few minor errors; correct use of irregular verbs	Some minor errors; use of irregular verbs	Several minor errors; little use of irregular verbs	Many errors; weak use of irregular verbs	Numerous errors; no use of irregular verbs

Rubric	5	4	3	2	1
Focus/Ideas	Strong composition; compares and contrasts effectively	Good composition; compares and contrasts	Reasonably good composition; compares and contrasts adequately	Weak composition; poorly compares and/or contrasts	Poor composition; neither compares nor contrasts
Organization	Similarities and differences in clear order; includes strong concluding statement	Similarities and differences in fairly clear order; includes well-developed conclusion	Similarities and differences in adequately clear order; includes adequate conclusion	Similarities and differences in confused order; vague or weak conclusion	No similarities and differences; no conclusion
Voice	Writer shows high interest in the subject	Writer shows interest in the subject	Writer shows some interest in the subject	Writer shows very little interest in the subject	Writer shows no interest in the subject
Word Choice	Strong use of compare/contrast words	Good use of compare/contrast words	Adequate use of compare/contrast words	Weak use of compare/contrast words	Poor or no use of compare/contrast words
Sentences	Sentences with different lengths and beginnings	Most sentences are of various lengths and beginnings	Some sentences are of various lengths and beginnings	Sentences with similar lengths and beginnings	No variety in sentence lengths and beginnings
Conventions	Few or no errors; strong use of irregular verbs	Few minor errors; correct use of irregular verbs	Some minor errors; use of irregular verbs	Many errors; weak use of irregular verbs	Numerous errors; no use of irregular verbs

Rubric	4	3	2	1
Focus/Ideas	Strong composition; compares and contrasts effectively	Good composition; compares and contrasts	Weak composition; poorly compares and/or contrasts	Poor composition; neither compares nor contrasts
Organization	Similarities and differences in clear order; includes strong concluding statement	Similarities and differences in fairly clear order; includes concluding statement	Similarities and differences in confused order; vague or weak conclusion	No similarities and differences; no conclusion
Voice	Writer shows interest in the subject	Writer shows some interest in the subject	Writer shows very little interest in the subject	Writer shows no interest in the subject
Word Choice	Strong use of compare/contrast words	Good use of compare/contrast words	Weak use of compare/contrast words	Poor or no use of compare/contrast words
Sentences	Sentences with different lengths and beginnings	Sentences with a few different lengths and beginnings	Sentences with similar lengths and beginnings	No variety in sentence lengths and beginnings
Conventions	Few or no errors; strong use of irregular verbs	Several minor errors; use of irregular verbs	Many errors; weak use of irregular verbs	Numerous errors; no use of irregular verbs

Rubric	6	5	4	3	2	1
Focus/Ideas	Clear statement and support of author's purpose	Mostly clear statement and support of author's purpose	Adequate statement and support of author's purpose	Occasionally clear statement and author's purpose	Somewhat unclear statement and support of author's purpose	Unclear statement and support of author's purpose
Organization	Contains clear main idea and details	Contains mostly clear main idea and some details	Contains adequate main idea and some details	Main idea somewhat clear; few details	Main idea somewhat unclear; little supporting details	Unclear main idea; no supporting details
Voice	Persuasive and knowledgeable	Mostly persuasive and knowledgeable	Reasonably persuasive; adequate knowledge	Sincere but not very persuasive; somewhat knowledgeable	Tries to be persuasive; rarely knowledgeable	Not persuasive; not knowledgeable
Word Choice	Uses persuasive language	Mostly uses persuasive language	Uses some persuasive language	Attempts to use persuasive language	Uses little persuasive language	Uses no persuasive language
Sentences	Clear and complete	Mostly clear and complete	Generally clear and complete	Somewhat clear and complete	Somewhat unclear and incomplete	Unclear and incomplete
Conventions	Few or no errors in use of singular and plural pronouns	Few errors in use of singular and plural pronouns	Some errors in use of singular and plural pronouns	Several major errors in use of singular and plural pronouns	Numerous errors in use of singular and plural pronouns	Consistently incorrect use of singular and plural pronouns

Rubric	5	4	3	2	1
Focus/Ideas	Clear statement and support of author's purpose	Mostly clear statement and support of author's purpose	Adequate statement and support of author's purpose	Somewhat unclear statement and support of author's purpose	Unclear statement and support of author's purpose
Organization	Contains clear main idea and details	Contains mostly clear main idea and some details	Contains adequate main idea and some details	Main idea somewhat unclear; little supporting details	Unclear main idea; no supporting details
Voice	Persuasive and knowledgeable	Mostly persuasive and knowledgeable	Reasonably persuasive; adequate knowledge	Tries to be persuasive; rarely knowledgeable	Not persuasive; not knowledgeable
Word Choice	Uses persuasive language	Mostly uses persuasive language	Uses some persuasive language	Uses little persuasive language	Uses no persuasive language
Sentences	Clear and complete	Mostly clear and complete	Generally clear and complete	Somewhat unclear and incomplete	Unclear and incomplete
Conventions	Few or no errors in use of singular and plural pronouns	Few errors in use of singular and plural pronouns	Some errors in use of singular and plural pronouns	Several errors in use of singular and plural pronouns	Consistently incorrect use of singular and plural pronouns

Rubric	4	3	2	1
Focus/Ideas	Clear statement and support of author's purpose	Mostly clear statement and support of author's purpose	Somewhat clear statement and support of author's purpose	Unclear statement and support of author's purpose
Organization	Contains clear main idea and details	Contains mostly clear main idea and some details	Main idea somewhat unclear; few details	Unclear main idea; no supporting details
Voice	Persuasive and knowledgeable	Somewhat persuasive; somewhat knowledgeable	Tries to be persuasive; rarely knowledgeable	Not persuasive; not knowledgeable
Word Choice	Uses persuasive language	Uses some persuasive language	Uses little persuasive language	Uses no persuasive language
Sentences	Clear and complete	Mostly clear and complete	Somewhat clear and complete	Unclear and incomplete
Conventions	Few or no errors in use of singular and plural pronouns	Moderate errors in use of singular and plural pronouns	Several errors in use of singular of plural pronouns	Consistently incorrect use of singular and plural pronouns

Rubric	6	5	4	3	2	1
Focus/Ideas	Vivid story, well-developed characters, detailed setting, plot building to climax	Good story, developed characters and setting, and plot	Story with adequate characters, setting, and plot development	Has somewhat of a plot; underdeveloped setting and characters	Story lacks focus, developed characters, detailed setting, and plot development	No focus or development of characters, setting, or plot
Organization	Clear beginning, middle, and end; clear sequence of events	Good beginning, middle and end; mostly clear sequence of events	Beginning, middle, and end; able to follow sequence of events	Unclear beginning, middle, or end; somewhat unclear sequence of events	Unclear beginning, middle and end; unclear sequence of events	No beginning, middle, or end; no sequence of events
Voice	Effective use of dialogue helps develop characters	Mostly effective use of dialogue	Adequate use of dialogue	Some effective use of dialogue	Dialogue often flat and ineffective	No dialogue used
Word Choice	Strong use of vivid, precise words	Good use of vivid, precise words	Some use of precise words	Attempt to use precise words	Few precise words	Vague, general words
Sentences	Clear sentences of various lengths and types; strong variety of beginnings	Most sentences are of various lengths and types; good variety of beginnings	Some sentences are of various lengths and types; some variety of beginnings	Sentences of a few lengths and types; little variety of beginnings	Sentences of similar length and type; weak variety of beginnings	No attempt at sentences of various lengths and types; no variety of beginnings
Conventions	Few, if any, errors; correct use of subject and object pronouns	Few minor errors; mostly correct use of subject and object pronouns	Some minor errors; some correct use of subject and object pronouns	Several minor errors; a few errors in use of subject and object pronouns	Many errors; several errors in use of subject and object pronouns	Numerous errors; incorrect use of subject and object pronouns

Rubric	5	4	3	2	1
Focus/Ideas	Vivid story, well-developed characters, detailed setting, plot building to climax	Good story, developed characters and setting, and plot	Story with adequate characters, setting, and plot development	Story lacks focus, developed characters, detailed setting, and plot development	No focus or development of characters, setting, or plot
Organization	Clear beginning, middle, and end; clear sequence of events	Good beginning, middle and end; mostly clear sequence of events	Beginning, middle, and end; able to follow sequence of events	Unclear beginning, middle and end; unclear sequence of events	No beginning, middle, or end; no sequence of events
Voice	Effective use of dialogue helps develop characters	Mostly effective use of dialogue	Adequate use of dialogue	Dialogue often flat and ineffective	No dialogue used
Word Choice	Strong use of vivid, precise words	Good use of vivid, precise words	Some use of precise words	Few precise words	Vague, general words
Sentences	Clear sentences of various lengths and types; strong variety of beginnings	Most sentences are of various lengths and types; good variety of beginnings	Some sentences are of various lengths and types; some variety of beginnings	Sentences of similar length and type; weak variety of beginnings	No attempt at sentences of various lengths and types; no variety of beginnings
Conventions	Few, if any, errors; correct use of subject and object pronouns	Few minor errors; mostly correct use of subject and object pronouns	Some minor errors; some correct use of subject and object pronouns	Many errors; several errors in use of subject and object pronouns	Numerous errors; incorrect use of subject and object pronouns

Rubric	4	3	2	1
Focus/Ideas	Vivid story, well-developed characters, detailed setting, plot building to climax	Story with adequate characters, setting, and plot development	Story lacks focus, developed characters, detailed setting, and plot development	No focus or development of characters, setting, or plot
Organization	Clear beginning, middle, and end; clear sequence of events	Beginning, middle, and end; able to follow sequence of events	Unclear beginning, middle and end; unclear sequence of events	No beginning, middle, or end; no sequence of events
Voice	Effective use of dialogue helps develop characters	Some effective use of dialogue	Dialogue often flat and ineffective	No dialogue used
Word Choice	Strong use of vivid, precise words	Some use of precise words	Few precise words	Vague, general words
Sentences	Clear sentences of various lengths and types; strong variety of beginnings	Sentences of a few lengths and types; variety of beginnings	Sentences of similar length and type; weak variety of beginnings	No attempt at sentences of various lengths and types; no variety of beginnings
Conventions	Few, if any, errors; correct use of subject and object pronouns	Several minor errors; correct use of subject and object pronouns	Many errors; a few errors in use of subject and object pronouns	Numerous errors; incorrect use of subject and object pronouns

Rubric	6	5	4	3	2	1
Focus/Ideas	Well-developed characters, setting, and events	Developed characters, setting, and events	Adequately developed characters, setting, and events	Somewhat underdeveloped characters, setting, and events	Underdeveloped characters, setting, and events	Undeveloped characters, setting, and events
Organization	Clear sequence of events	Able to follow sequence of events	Adequate sequence of events	Attempt at sequence of events	Unclear sequence of events	No sequence of events
Voice	Clear interest in talents and important events in subject's life	Interest in talents and important events in subject's life	Some interest in talents and important events in subject's life	Tries to show interest in talents and important events in subject's life	Little interest in talents and important events in subject's life	No interest in talents and important events in subject's life
Word Choice	Strong use of vivid words	Good use of vivid words	Adequate use of vivid words	Attempt to use vivid words	Weak use of vivid words	No use of vivid words
Sentences	Clear sentences of various lengths and types; strong variety of sentence beginnings	Most sentences are of various lengths and types; good variety of sentence beginnings	Some variety in sentence lengths and types; some variety of sentence beginnings	Sentences of a few lengths and types; little variety of sentence beginnings	Sentences of similar length and type; weak variety of sentence beginnings	No attempt at sentences of various lengths and types; no variety of sentence beginnings
Conventions	Few, if any, errors; strong use of possessive pronouns	Few minor errors; mostly correct use of possessive pronouns	Some minor errors; some correct use of possessive pronouns	Several minor errors; little use of possessive pronouns	Many errors; weak use of possessive pronouns	Numerous errors; no or incorrect use of possessive pronouns

Rubric	5	4	3	2	1
Focus/Ideas	Well-developed characters, setting, and events	Developed characters, setting, and events	Adequately developed characters, setting, and events	Underdeveloped characters, setting, and events	Undeveloped characters, setting, and events
Organization	Clear sequence of events	Able to follow sequence of events	Adequate sequence of events	Unclear sequence of events	No sequence of events
Voice	Clear interest in talents and important events in subject's life	Interest in talents and important events in subject's life	Some interest in talents and important events in subject's life	Little interest in talents and important events in subject's life	No interest in talents and important events in subject's life
Word Choice	Strong use of vivid words	Good use of vivid words	Adequate use of vivid words	Weak use of vivid words	No use of vivid words
Sentences	Clear sentences of various lengths and types; strong variety of sentence beginnings	Most sentences are of various lengths and types; good variety of sentence beginnings	Some variety in sentence lengths and types; some variety of sentence beginnings	Sentences of similar length and type; weak variety of sentence beginnings	No attempt at sentences of various lengths and types; no variety of sentence beginnings
Conventions	Few, if any, errors; strong use of possessive pronouns	Few minor errors; mostly correct use of possessive pronouns	Some minor errors; some correct use of possessive pronouns	Many errors; weak use of possessive pronouns	Numerous errors; no or incorrect use of possessive pronouns

Rubric	4	3	2	1
Focus/Ideas	Well-developed characters, setting, and events	Developed characters, setting, and events	Underdeveloped characters, setting, and events	Undeveloped characters, setting, and events
Organization	Clear sequence of events	Able to follow sequence of events	Unclear sequence of events	No sequence of events
Voice	Clear interest in talents and important events in subject's life	Some interest in talents and important events in subject's life	Little interest in talents and important events in subject's life	No interest in talents and important events in subject's life
Word Choice	Strong use of vivid words	Adequate use of vivid words	Weak use of vivid words	No use of vivid words
Sentences	Clear sentences of various lengths and types; strong variety of sentence beginnings	Sentences of a few lengths and types; variety of sentence beginnings	Sentences of similar length and type; weak variety of sentence beginnings	No attempt at sentences of various lengths and types; no variety of sentence beginnings
Conventions	Few, if any, errors; strong use of possessive pronouns	Several minor errors; use of possessive pronouns	Many errors; weak use of possessive pronouns	Numerous errors; no or incorrect use of possessive pronouns

Rubric	6	5	4	3	2	1
Focus/Ideas	Clear, focused autobiography with many supporting details	Most ideas in autobiography clear and supported	Ideas in autobiography adequately clear and supported	Somewhat clear ideas and some support	Some ideas in autobiography off topic	Autobiography with no clarity or development
Organization	Organized logically into paragraphs; follows a clear sequence	Organized logically, with generally strong paragraphs; sequence is mostly clear	Organized adequately with somewhat strong paragraphs; sequence is fairly clear	Attempt to organize into paragraphs, and somewhat clear; sequence somewhat unclear	Attempt to organize into paragraphs, but not clearly; weak sequence	No apparent organizational pattern in use of paragraphs or sequence
Voice	Engaging; shows writer's feeling about subject	Evident voice connecting with reader	Some evidence of writer's feelings about the subject	Feelings about subject somewhat unclear	Weak voice	Flat writing with no identifiable voice
Word Choice	Vivid, precise word choice	Good word choice	Accurate word choice	Few precise words	Limited or repetitive word choice	Incorrect or very limited word choice
Sentences	Varied sentences in logical progression	Not as varied; order mostly logical	Some varied sentences in adequate order	Too many similar sentences	No variety	Many fragments and run-ons
Conventions	Excellent control and accuracy; contractions used correctly	Good control, few errors; contractions mostly used correctly	Fair control; contractions used adequately	Limited control; attempt to use contractions	Weak control; contractions used incorrectly	Serious errors that obscure meaning

Rubric	5	4	3	2	1
Focus/Ideas	Clear, focused autobiography with many supporting details	Most ideas in autobiography clear and supported	Ideas in autobiography adequately clear and supported	Some ideas in autobiography off topic	Autobiography with no clarity or development
Organization	Organized logically into paragraphs; follows a clear sequence	Organized logically, with generally strong paragraphs; sequence is mostly clear	Organized adequately with somewhat strong paragraphs; sequence is fairly clear	Attempt to organize into paragraphs, but not clearly; weak sequence	No apparent organizational pattern in use of paragraphs or sequence
Voice	Engaging; shows writer's feeling about subject	Evident voice connecting with reader	Some evidence of writer's feelings about the subject	Weak voice	Flat writing with no identifiable voice
Word Choice	Vivid, precise word choice	Good word choice	Accurate word choice	Limited or repetitive word choice	Incorrect or very limited word choice
Sentences	Varied sentences in logical progression	Not as varied; order mostly logical	Some varied sentences in adequate order	No variety	Many fragments and run-ons
Conventions	Excellent control and accuracy; contractions used correctly	Good control, few errors; contractions mostly used correctly	Fair control; contractions used adequately	Weak control; contractions used incorrectly	Serious errors that obscure meaning

Rubric	4	3	2	1
Focus/Ideas	Clear, focused autobiography with many supporting details	Most ideas in autobiography clear and supported	Some ideas in autobiography unclear or off topic	Autobiography with no clarity or development
Organization	Organized logically into paragraphs; follows a clear sequence	Organized logically, with generally strong paragraphs; sequence is fairly clear	Attempt to organize into paragraphs, but not clearly; weak sequence	No apparent organizational pattern in use of paragraphs or sequence
Voice	Engaging; shows writer's feeling about subject	Evident voice connecting with reader	Weak voice	Flat writing with no identifiable voice
Word Choice	Vivid, precise word choice	Accurate word choice	Limited or repetitive word choice	Incorrect or very limited word choice
Sentences	Varied sentences in logical progression	Not as varied; order mostly logical	Too many similar sentences	Many fragments and run-ons
Conventions	Excellent control and accuracy; contractions used correctly	Good control, few errors; contractions mostly used correctly	Weak control; contractions used incorrectly	Serious errors that obscure meaning

Rubric	6	5	4	3	2	1
Focus/Ideas	Strong summary; only uses important information	Good summary; mostly uses important information	Reasonably good summary; uses some important information	Somewhat good summary; uses many details	Summary has some main ideas and too many details	Does not understand summary form
Organization	Important ideas are in correct sequence	Sequence of events described mainly in clear order	Sequence of events is generally correct	Sequence of events logical with some lapses	Sequence of events isn't always clear	No clear sequence of events
Voice	Shows understanding of the main ideas	Shows understanding of topic	Shows general understanding of topic	Understanding of topic uneven	Lacks understanding of topic	Does not understand topic
Word Choice	Uses strong action verbs and time-order words	Uses mostly strong action verbs and time-order words	Adequate use of action verbs and time-order words	Attempts to use action verbs and time-order words	Few or no strong verbs or time-order words	Poor word choice
Sentences	Clear sentences of different lengths and types	Most sentences are of different lengths and types	Some sentences are of different lengths and types	Sentences of a few different lengths and types	Sentences of similar length and type	No variety of sentence length and type
Conventions	Few, if any, errors; correct use of prepositions	Few minor errors; mostly correct use of prepositions	Some minor errors; use of prepositions	Several minor errors; little use of prepositions	Many errors; weak use of prepositions	Many serious errors; incorrect or no use of prepositions

Rubric	5	4	3	2	1
Focus/Ideas	Strong summary; only uses important information	Good summary; mostly uses important information	Reasonably good summary; uses some important information	Summary has some main ideas and too many details	Does not understand summary form
Organization	Important ideas are in correct sequence	Sequence of events described mainly in clear order	Sequence of events is generally correct	Sequence of events isn't always clear	No clear sequence of events
Voice	Shows understanding of the main ideas	Shows understanding of topic	Shows general understanding of topic	Lacks understanding of topic	Does not understand topic
Word Choice	Uses strong action verbs and time-order words	Uses mostly strong action verbs and time-order words	Adequate use of action verbs and time-order words	Few or no strong verbs or time-order words	Poor word choice
Sentences	Clear sentences of different lengths and types	Most sentences are of different lengths and types	Some sentences are of different lengths and types	Sentences of similar length and type	No variety of sentence length and type
Conventions	Few, if any, errors; correct use of prepositions	Few minor errors; mostly correct use of prepositions	Some minor errors; use of prepositions	Many errors; weak use of prepositions	Many serious errors; incorrect or no use of prepositions

Rubric	4	3	2	1
Focus/Ideas	Strong summary; only uses important information	Good summary; mostly uses important information	Summary has some main ideas and too many details	Does not understand summary form
Organization	Important ideas are in correct sequence	Sequence of events is generally correct	Sequence of events isn't always clear	No clear sequence of events
Voice	Shows understanding of the main ideas	Shows understanding of topic	Lacks understanding of topic	Does not understand topic
Word Choice	Uses strong action verbs and time-order words	Uses some strong action verbs and time-order words	Few or no strong verbs or time-order words	Poor word choice
Sentences	Clear sentences of different lengths and types	Sentences of a few lengths and types	Sentences of similar length and type	No variety of sentence length and type
Conventions	Few, if any, errors; correct use of prepositions	Several small errors; use of prepositions	Many errors; weak use of prepositions	Many serious errors; incorrect or no use of prepositions

Rubric	6	5	4	3	2	1
Focus/Ideas	Clear, logical main idea; many supporting details; nonfiction	Clear main idea; some supporting details; nonfiction	Reasonably clear main idea; few supporting details; nonfiction	Somewhat unclear main idea; limited details; somewhat like fictions	Unclear, illogical main idea; no details; seems like fiction	No main idea; no supporting details; fiction
Organization	Correct use of letter	Mostly correct use of letter	A few mistakes in letter format	Attempt to use letter format	Many mistakes in letter format	No attempt to use letter format
Voice	Clear, strong position; writer's personality clearly conveyed	Position conveyed; sense of writer's personality	Position mostly conveyed; some sense of writer's personality	Attempts to show position and writer's personality	Weak position; weak sense of writer's personality	No position; no sense of writer's personality
Word Choice	Strong use of persuasive language	Mostly uses persuasive language	Reasonable use of persuasive language	Attempts to use persuasive language	Weak use of persuasive language	Informal, unpersuasive language
Sentences	Clear sentences of various lengths and types; strong variety of sentence beginnings	Most sentences are of various lengths and types; variety of sentence beginnings	Some sentences are of various lengths and types; some variety of sentence beginnings	Sentences of a few lengths and types; little variety of sentence beginnings	Sentences of similar length and type; weak variety of sentence beginnings	No attempt at sentences of various lengths and types; no variety of sentence beginnings
Conventions	Few, if any, errors; strong use of adjectives and articles; complete sentences	Few errors; good use of adjectives and articles; mostly complete sentences	Some errors; use of adjectives and articles; sentences generally complete	Several errors; little use of adjectives and articles; some complete sentences	Many errors; weak use of adjectives and articles; few complete sentences	Numerous errors; no or incorrect use of adjectives and articles; no complete sentences

Rubric	5	4	3	2	1
Focus/Ideas	Clear, logical main idea; many supporting details; nonfiction	Clear main idea; some supporting details; nonfiction	Reasonably clear main idea; few supporting details; nonfiction	Unclear, illogical main idea; no details; seems like fiction	No main idea; no supporting details; fiction
Organization	Correct use of letter	Mostly correct use of letter	A few mistakes in letter format	Many mistakes in letter format	No attempt to use letter format
Voice	Clear, strong position; writer's personality clearly conveyed	Position conveyed; sense of writer's personality	Position mostly conveyed; some sense of writer's personality	Weak position; weak sense of writer's personality	No position; no sense of writer's personality
Word Choice	Strong use of persuasive language	Mostly uses persuasive language	Reasonable use of persuasive language	Weak use of persuasive language	Informal, unpersuasive language
Sentences	Clear sentences of various lengths and types; strong variety of sentence beginnings	Most sentences are of various lengths and types; variety of sentence beginnings	Some sentences are of various lengths and types; some variety of sentence beginnings	Sentences of similar length and type; weak variety of sentence beginnings	No attempt at sentences of various lengths and types; no variety of sentence beginnings
Conventions	Few, if any, errors; strong use of adjectives and articles; complete sentences	Few errors; good use of adjectives and articles; mostly complete sentences	Some errors; use of adjectives and articles; sentences generally complete	Many errors; weak use of adjectives and articles; few complete sentences	Numerous errors; no or incorrect use of adjectives and articles; no complete sentences

Rubric	4	3	2	1
Focus/Ideas	Clear, logical main idea; many supporting details; nonfiction	Clear main idea; some supporting details; nonfiction	Unclear, illogical main idea; few supporting details; seems like fiction	No main idea; no supporting details; fiction
Organization	Correct use of letter	A few mistakes in letter format	Many mistakes in letter format	No attempt to use letter format
Voice	Clear, strong position; writer's personality clearly conveyed	Position conveyed; sense of writer's personality	Weak position; weak sense of writer's personality	No position; no sense of writer's personality
Word Choice	Strong use of persuasive language	Some use of persuasive language	Weak use of persuasive language	Informal, unpersuasive language
Sentences	Clear sentences of various lengths and types; strong variety of sentence beginnings	Sentences of a few lengths and types; variety of sentence beginnings	Sentences of similar length and type; weak variety of sentence beginnings	No attempt at sentences of various lengths and types; no variety of sentence beginnings
Conventions	Few, if any, errors; strong use of adjectives and articles; complete sentences	Several minor errors; use of adjectives and articles; mostly complete sentences	Many errors; weak use of adjectives and articles; few complete sentences	Numerous errors; no or incorrect use of adjectives and articles; no complete sentences

PERSONAL NARRATIVE

Rubric	6	5	4	3	2	1
Focus/Ideas	Focuses on specific, real memory; told from writer's point of view	Includes events from writer's memory; told from writer's point of view	Includes reasonable events from writer's memory; told from writer's point of view	Includes some events from writer's memory; mostly told from writer's point of view	Includes few events from writer's memory; sometimes told from writer's point of view	Narrative does not focus on real events from writer's memory
Organization	Clear order of events	Mostly clear order of events	Can reasonably follow order of events	Can follow order of events	Unclear order of events	No order of events
Voice	Writer shows strong personal emotions and thoughts	Writer shows personal emotions and thoughts	Writer shows some personal emotions and thoughts	Writer shows few personal emotions and thoughts	Writer shows little personal emotions and thoughts	Writer makes no effort to show personal emotions and thoughts
Word Choice	Strong use of verbs and adjectives to bring the story to life	Good use of verbs and adjectives	Some verbs and adjective	Attempt at using verbs and adjectives	Poor use of verbs and adjectives; story lacks description	No effort made to use verbs and adjectives
Sentences	Clear sentences of different lengths and types	Most sentences are of various lengths and types	Some sentences are of various lengths and types	Sentences of a few lengths and types	Sentences of similar length and type	No variety of sentence length and type
Conventions	Few, if any, errors; correct use of verbs and adjectives	Few errors; mostly correct use of verbs and adjectives	Some minor errors; use of verbs and adjectives	Several minor errors; limited use of verbs and adjectives	Many errors; weak use of verbs and adjectives	Many serious errors; incorrect or no use of verbs and adjectives

Rubric	5	4	3	2	1
Focus/Ideas	Focuses on specific, real memory; told from writer's point of view	Includes events from writer's memory; told from writer's point of view	Includes reasonable events from writer's memory; told from writer's point of view	Includes few events from writer's memory; sometimes told from writer's point of view	Narrative does not focus on real events from writer's memory
Organization	Clear order of events	Mostly clear order of events	Can reasonably follow order of events	Unclear order of events	No order of events
Voice	Writer shows strong personal emotions and thoughts	Writer shows personal emotions and thoughts	Writer shows some personal emotions and thoughts	Writer shows little personal emotions and thoughts	Writer makes no effort to show personal emotions and thoughts
Word Choice	Strong use of verbs and adjectives to bring the story to life	Good use of verbs and adjectives	Some verbs and adjective	Poor use of verbs and adjectives; story lacks description	No effort made to use verbs and adjectives
Sentences	Clear sentences of different lengths and types	Most sentences are of various lengths and types	Some sentences are of various lengths and types	Sentences of similar length and type	No variety of sentence length and type
Conventions	Few, if any, errors; correct use of verbs and adjectives	Few errors; mostly correct use of verbs and adjectives	Some minor errors; use of verbs and adjectives	Many errors; weak use of verbs and adjectives	Many serious errors; incorrect or no use of verbs and adjectives

Rubric	4	3	2	1
Focus/Ideas	Focuses on specific, real memory; told from writer's point of view	Includes events from writer's memory; told from writer's point of view	Includes some events from writer's memory; mostly told from writer's point of view	Narrative does not focus on real events from writer's memory
Organization	Clear order of events	Can follow order of events	Unclear order of events	No order of events
Voice	Writer shows personal emotions and thoughts	Writer shows some personal emotions and thoughts	Writer shows few personal emotions and thoughts	Writer makes no effort to show personal emotions and thoughts
Word Choice	Strong use of verbs and adjectives to bring the story to life	Good try at using verbs and adjectives	Poor use of verbs and adjectives; story lacks description	No effort made to use verbs and adjectives
Sentences	Clear sentences of different lengths and types	Sentences of a few lengths and types	Sentences of similar length and type	No variety of sentence length and type
Conventions	Few, if any, errors; correct use of verbs and adjectives	Several small errors; use of verbs and adjectives	Many errors; weak use of verbs and adjectives	Many serious errors; incorrect or no use of verbs and adjectives

FREE VERSE POETRY

Rubric	6	5	4	3	2	1
Focus/Ideas	Vivid, well-developed narrative	Good narrative	Good narrative with adequate development	Somewhat developed narrative	Narrative lacking focus	Narrative with no focus
Organization	Correct use of free verse format (no set structure or rhyme scheme)	Mostly correct use of free verse format	Adequate use of free verse format	Attempt to use free verse format	Incorrect use of free verse format	No attempt at using free verse format
Voice	Clear, distinct, engaging voice	Mostly clear, distinct, engaging voice	Adequately clear, distinct, engaging voice	Somewhat clear, distinct, engaging voice	Unclear, indistinct, unengaging voice	No attempt to create a clear, distinct, engaging voice
Word Choice	Strong use of exact nouns, vivid verbs, and figurative language, including similes, metaphors, and sensory details	Good use of exact nouns, vivid verbs, and figurative language, including similes, metaphors, and sensory details	Some use of exact nouns, vivid verbs, and figurative language, including similes, metaphors, and sensory details	Attempt at using exact nouns, vivid verbs, and figurative language, including similes, metaphors, and sensory details	Weak use of exact nouns, vivid verbs, and figurative language, including similes, metaphors, and sensory details	Little or no use of exact nouns, vivid verbs, and figurative language, including similes, metaphors, and sensory details
Sentences	Clear sentences of various lengths and types	Mostly clear sentences of various lengths and types	Some sentences of various lengths and types	Sentences of a few lengths and types	Sentences of similar length and type	No attempt at sentences of various lengths and types
Conventions	Few, if any, errors; strong use of adverbs	Few minor errors; good use of adverbs	Some minor errors; use of adverbs	Several minor errors; some adverbs used correctly	Many errors; weak use of adverbs	Numerous errors, no use of adverbs

Rubric	5	4	3	2	1
Focus/Ideas	Vivid, well-developed narrative	Good narrative	Good narrative with adequate development	Narrative lacking focus	Narrative with no focus
Organization	Correct use of free verse format (no set structure or rhyme scheme)	Mostly correct use of free verse format	Adequate use of free verse format	Incorrect use of free verse format	No attempt at using free verse format
Voice	Clear, distinct, engaging voice	Mostly clear, distinct, engaging voice	Adequately clear, distinct, engaging voice	Unclear, indistinct, unengaging voice	No attempt to create a clear, distinct, engaging voice
Word Choice	Strong use of exact nouns, vivid verbs, and figurative language, including similes, metaphors, and sensory details	Good use of exact nouns, vivid verbs, and figurative language, including similes, metaphors, and sensory details	Some use of exact nouns, vivid verbs, and figurative language, including similes, metaphors, and sensory details	Weak use of exact nouns, vivid verbs, and figurative language, including similes, metaphors, and sensory details	Little or no use of exact nouns, vivid verbs, and figurative language, including similes, metaphors, and sensory details
Sentences	Clear sentences of various lengths and types	Mostly clear sentences of various lengths and types	Some sentences of various lengths and types	Sentences of similar length and type	No attempt at sentences of various lengths and types
Conventions	Few, if any, errors; strong use of adverbs	Few minor errors; good use of adverbs	Some minor errors; use of adverbs	Many errors; weak use of adverbs	Numerous errors, no use of adverbs

Rubric	4	3	2	1
Focus/Ideas	Vivid, well-developed narrative	Good narrative with adequate development	Narrative lacking focus	Narrative with no focus
Organization	Correct use of free verse format (no set structure or rhyme scheme)	Some use of free verse format	Incorrect use of free verse format	No attempt at using free verse format
Voice	Clear, distinct, engaging voice	Somewhat clear, distinct, engaging voice	Unclear, indistinct, unengaging voice	No attempt to create a clear, distinct, engaging voice
Word Choice	Strong use of exact nouns, vivid verbs, and figurative language, including similes, metaphors, and sensory details	Some use of exact nouns, vivid verbs, and figurative language, including similes, metaphors, and sensory details	Weak use of exact nouns, vivid verbs, and figurative language, including similes, metaphors, and sensory details	Little or no use of exact nouns, vivid verbs, and figurative language, including similes, metaphors, and sensory details
Sentences	Clear sentences of various lengths and types	Sentences of a few lengths and types	Sentences of similar length and type	No attempt at sentences of various lengths and types
Conventions	Few, if any, errors; strong use of adverbs	Several minor errors; use of adverbs	Many errors; weak use of adverbs	Numerous errors, no use of adverbs

INVITATION

Rubric	6	5	4	3	2	1
Focus/Ideas	Clear focus and purpose for invitation	Fairly clear focus and purpose for invitation	Reasonably clear focus and purpose for invitation	Somewhat unclear focus and purpose for invitation	Unclear focus and purpose for invitation	No attempt made to offer a reason for the event
Organization	Clearly organized details, such as date, time, and location of party	Fairly clear details, such as date, time, and location of party	Reasonably clear details, such as date, time, and location of party	Somewhat able to follow details, such as date, time, and location of party	Effort to include details, such as date, time, and location; details for party are unclear	No effort made to include party details, such as date, time, and location
Voice	Writer achieves an animated voice and makes the party sound enticing	Writer has an animated voice and inviting tone	Writer has a reasonably animated voice and inviting tone	Some evidence of animated voice and inviting tone	Attempts an animated voice and inviting tone	No attempt at an animated voice or inviting tone
Word Choice	Strong use of vivid words	Good use of vivid words	Some vivid words	Few vivid words	Weak use of vivid words	No use of vivid words
Sentences	Clear sentences of various lengths and types	Most sentences of various lengths and types	Some sentences of various lengths and types	Sentences of a few lengths and types	No sentences; little attempt at various lengths and types of sentences	No attempt at sentences; no attempt at various lengths and types of sentences
Conventions	Few, if any, errors; correct use of comparative and superlative adverbs	Few minor errors; mostly correct use of comparative and superlative adverbs	Some minor errors; adequate use of comparative and superlative adverbs	Several minor errors; little use of comparative and superlative adverbs	Many errors; inaccurate use of comparative and superlative adverbs	Numerous errors; no use of comparative and superlative adverbs

Rubric	5	4	3	2	1
Focus/Ideas	Clear focus and purpose for invitation	Fairly clear focus and purpose for invitation	Reasonably clear focus and purpose for invitation	Unclear focus and purpose for invitation	No attempt made to offer a reason for the event
Organization	Clearly organized details, such as date, time, and location of party	Fairly clear details, such as date, time, and location of party	Reasonably clear details, such as date, time, and location of party	Effort to include details, such as date, time, and location; details for party are unclear	No effort made to include party details, such as date, time, and location
Voice	Writer achieves an animated voice and makes the party sound enticing	Writer has an animated voice and inviting tone	Writer has a reasonably animated voice and inviting tone	Attempts an animated voice and inviting tone	No attempt at an animated voice or inviting tone
Word Choice	Strong use of vivid words	Good use of vivid words	Some vivid words	Weak use of vivid words	No use of vivid words
Sentences	Clear sentences of various lengths and types	Most sentences of various lengths and types	Some sentences of various lengths and types	No sentences; little attempt at various lengths and types of sentences	No attempt at sentences; no attempt at various lengths and types of sentences
Conventions	Few, if any, errors; correct use of comparative and superlative adverbs	Few minor errors; mostly correct use of comparative and superlative adverbs	Some minor errors; adequate use of comparative and superlative adverbs	Many errors; inaccurate use of comparative and superlative adverbs	Numerous errors; no use of comparative and superlative adverbs

Rubric	4	3	2	1
Focus/Ideas	Clear focus and purpose for invitation	Fairly clear focus and purpose for invitation	Unclear focus and purpose for invitation	No attempt made to offer a reason for the event
Organization	Clearly organized details, such as date, time, and location of party	Able to follow details, such as date, time, and location of party	Effort to include details, such as date, time, and location; details for party are unclear	No effort made to include party details, such as date, time, and location
Voice	Writer achieves an animated voice and makes the party sound enticing	Some evidence of animated voice and inviting tone	Attempts an animated voice and inviting tone	No attempt at an animated voice or inviting tone
Word Choice	Strong use of vivid words	Adequate use of vivid words	Weak use of vivid words	No use of vivid words
Sentences	Clear sentences of various lengths and types	Sentences of a few lengths and types	No sentences; little attempt at various lengths and types of sentences	No attempt at sentences; no attempt at various lengths and types of sentences
Conventions	Few, if any, errors; correct use of comparative and superlative adverbs	Several minor errors; mostly correct use of comparative and superlative adverbs	Many errors; inaccurate use of comparative and superlative adverbs	Numerous errors; no use of comparative and superlative adverbs

Rubric	6	5	4	3	2	1
Focus/Ideas	Clear, focused review with many supporting details	Most ideas in review clear and supported	Some ideas in review clear and supported	Few ideas in review clear and supported	Some ideas in review unclear or off topic	Review with no clarity or development
Organization	Organized logically, no gaps; clearly presented book topic	Organized logically, one or two gaps; book topic presented	Organized logically, few gaps; book topic presented	Organizational pattern attempted but not clear; book topic somewhat unclear	Organizational pattern attempted but not clear; book topic unclear	No organizational pattern evident; book topic not presented clearly
Voice	Engaging; shows writer's feelings/opinion about subject	Mostly engaging; mostly shows writer's feelings/opinion about subject	Evident voice connecting with reader; shows writer's feelings	Voice sometimes connects with reader; somewhat shows writer's feelings	Weak voice; weak display of writer's feelings/opinion about subject	Flat writing with no voice; writer doesn't state his/her opinion
Word Choice	Vivid, precise word choice	Good use choice	Accurate word choice	Limited word choice	Repetitive word choice	Incorrect or very limited word choice
Sentences	Clear sentences of various lengths and types; correct punctuation	Most sentences of various lengths and types; mostly correct punctuation	Some sentences of various lengths and types; some correct punctuation	Sentences of a few lengths and types; attempt at correct punctuation	Sentences of similar length and type; weak use of punctuation	No attempt at sentences of various lengths or types; incorrect or no punctuation
Conventions	Few, if any, errors; correct use of conjunctions	Few minor errors; mostly correct use of conjunctions	Several minor errors; some correct use of conjunctions	Many errors; limited use of conjunctions	Major errors; weak use of conjunctions	Numerous errors; incorrect or no use of conjunctions

Rubric	5	4	3	2	1
Focus/Ideas	Clear, focused review with many supporting details	Most ideas in review clear and supported	Some ideas in review clear and supported	Some ideas in review unclear or off topic	Review with no clarity or development
Organization	Organized logically, no gaps; clearly presented book topic	Organized logically, one or two gaps; book topic presented	Organized logically, few gaps; book topic presented	Organizational pattern attempted but not clear; book topic unclear	No organizational pattern evident; book topic not presented clearly
Voice	Engaging; shows writer's feelings/opinion about subject	Mostly engaging; mostly shows writer's feelings/opinion about subject	Evident voice connecting with reader; shows writer's feelings	Weak voice; weak display of writer's feelings/opinion about subject	Flat writing with no voice; writer doesn't state his/her opinion
Word Choice	Vivid, precise word choice	Good use choice	Accurate word choice	Repetitive word choice	Incorrect or very limited word choice
Sentences	Clear sentences of various lengths and types; correct punctuation	Most sentences of various lengths and types; mostly correct punctuation	Some sentences of various lengths and types; some correct punctuation	Sentences of similar length and type; weak use of punctuation	No attempt at sentences of various lengths or types; incorrect or no punctuation
Conventions	Few, if any, errors; correct use of conjunctions	Few minor errors; mostly correct use of conjunctions	Several minor errors; some correct use of conjunctions	Major errors; weak use of conjunctions	Numerous errors; incorrect or no use of conjunctions

Rubric	4	3	2	1
Focus/Ideas	Clear, focused review with many supporting details	Most ideas in review clear and supported	Some ideas in review unclear or off topic	Review with no clarity or development
Organization	Organized logically, no gaps; clearly presented book topic	Organized logically, few gaps; book topic presented	Organizational pattern attempted but not clear; book topic unclear	No organizational pattern evident; book topic not presented clearly
Voice	Engaging; shows writer's feelings/opinion about subject	Evident voice connecting with reader; shows writer's feelings	Weak voice; weak display of writer's feelings/opinion about subject	Flat writing with no voice; writer doesn't state his/her opinion
Word Choice	Vivid, precise word choice	Accurate word choice	Limited or repetitive word choice	Incorrect or very limited word choice
Sentences	Clear sentences of various lengths and types; correct punctuation	Sentences of a few lengths and types; mostly correct punctuation	Sentences of similar length and type; weak use of punctuation	No attempt at sentences of various lengths or types; incorrect or no punctuation
Conventions	Few, if any, errors; correct use of conjunctions	Several minor errors; mostly correct use of conjunctions	Many errors; weak use of conjunctions	Numerous errors; incorrect or no use of conjunctions

Rubric	6	5	4	3	2	1
Focus/Ideas	Includes most important information from selection	Includes important information from selection	Includes adequate information from selection	Includes some important information from selection	Includes irrelevant information from selection	Does not include any important information from selection
Organization	Information is clear and orderly	Information is mostly clear and orderly	Information is reasonably clear and orderly	Information is somewhat clear and orderly	Information is unclear or disorderly	Information is neither clear nor orderly
Voice	Objective; no personal bias or opinions	Mostly objective; minimal personal bias or opinions	Reasonably objective; personal bias or opinions slightly present	Somewhat objective; some personal bias or opinions	Attempt to be objective; clear personal bias and opinions present	Not objective; too much bias or personal information
Word Choice	Avoids unnecessary words and information	Mostly avoids unnecessary words and information	Uses a few unnecessary words and information	Uses some unnecessary words and information	Uses many unnecessary words; vague information	Notes are wordy and irrelevant
Sentences	Uses clear, short sentences and sentence fragments	Mostly clear, short sentences and sentence fragments	Generally clear, short sentences and sentence fragments	Attempt to use clear, short sentences and sentence fragments	Mostly uses unclear and long sentences	Sentences are unclear or too long
Conventions	All proper nouns are capitalized	Most proper nouns are capitalized	Proper pronouns are generally capitalized	Some proper pronouns are capitalized	Few proper pronouns are capitalized	No proper pronouns are capitalized

Rubric	5	4	3	2	1
Focus/Ideas	Includes most important information from selection	Includes important information from selection	Includes some important information from selection	Includes irrelevant information from selection	Does not include any important information from selection
Organization	Information is clear and orderly	Information is mostly clear and orderly	Information is somewhat clear and orderly	Information is unclear or disorderly	Information is neither clear nor orderly
Voice	Objective; no personal bias or opinions	Mostly objective; minimal personal bias or opinions	Reasonably objective; some personal bias or opinions	Attempt to be objective; clear personal bias and opinions present	Not objective; too much bias or personal information
Word Choice	Avoids unnecessary words and information	Mostly avoids unnecessary words and information	Uses some unnecessary words and information	Uses many unnecessary words; vague information	Notes are wordy and irrelevant
Sentences	Uses clear, short sentences and sentence fragments	Mostly clear, short sentences and sentence fragments	Generally clear, short sentences and sentence fragments	Uses somewhat clear, short sentences and fragments	Sentences are unclear or too long
Conventions	All proper nouns are capitalized	Most proper nouns are capitalized	Some proper pronouns are capitalized	Few proper pronouns are capitalized	No proper pronouns are capitalized

Rubric	4	3	2	1
Focus/Ideas	Includes most important information from selection	Includes some important information from selection	Includes irrelevant information from selection	Does not include any important information from selection
Organization	Information is clear and orderly	Information is mostly clear and orderly	Information is somewhat clear and orderly	Information is neither clear nor orderly
Voice	Objective; no personal bias or opinions	Mostly objective; a little personal bias or opinions	Somewhat objective; some personal bias or opinions	Not objective; too much bias or personal information
Word Choice	Avoids unnecessary words and information	Uses some unnecessary words and information	Uses many unnecessary words; vague information	Notes are wordy and irrelevant
Sentences	Uses clear, short sentences and sentence fragments	Uses mostly clear, short sentences and sentence fragments	Uses somewhat clear, short sentences and fragments	Sentences are unclear or too long
Conventions	All proper nouns are capitalized	Most proper nouns are capitalized	Some proper nouns are capitalized	Few to no proper pronouns are capitalized

Rubric	6	5	4	3	2	1
Focus/Ideas	Clear, focused limerick	Mostly clear and focused limerick	Adequately clear and focused limerick	Few details in limerick unclear	Some details in limerick unclear	Limerick lacks clarity and development
Organization	Correct use of limerick structure	Mostly correct use of limerick structure	Adequate use of limerick structure	Some attempt to use limerick structure	Little attempt to use limerick structure	No attempt to use limerick structure
Voice	Engaged, lively voice throughout	Engaged, lively voice most of the time	Writer engaged with topic	Writer is somewhat engaged with topic	Writer not very engaged	Uninterested tone
Word Choice	Strong use of sensory details	Good use of sensory details	Some sensory details	Attempt to use sensory details	Weak use of sensory details	No use of sensory details
Sentences	Energetic; tied cleverly by rhythm and rhyme	Good balance between structure and rhyme scheme	Adequate balance between structure and rhyme scheme	Simple but mostly connected by rhyme	Simple and connected only by rhyme	Simple, error-filled; confused
Conventions	Few, if any, errors; correct use of abbreviations	Few minor errors; mostly correct use of abbreviations	Some minor errors; some correct use of abbreviations	Several minor errors; slight incorrect use of abbreviations	Many errors; incorrect use of abbreviations	Numerous errors; no use of abbreviations

Rubric	5	4	3	2	1
Focus/Ideas	Clear, focused limerick	Mostly clear and focused limerick	Adequately clear and focused limerick	Some details in limerick unclear	Limerick lacks clarity and development
Organization	Correct use of limerick structure	Mostly correct use of limerick structure	Adequate use of limerick structure	Little attempt to use limerick structure	No attempt to use limerick structure
Voice	Engaged, lively voice throughout	Engaged, lively voice most of the time	Writer engaged with topic	Writer not very engaged	Uninterested tone
Word Choice	Strong use of sensory details	Good use of sensory details	Adequate use of sensory details	Weak use of sensory details	No use of sensory details
Sentences	Energetic; tied cleverly by rhythm and rhyme	Good balance between structure and rhyme scheme	Adequate balance between structure and rhyme scheme	Simple and connected only by rhyme	Simple, error-filled; confused
Conventions	Few, if any, errors; correct use of abbreviations	Few minor errors; mostly correct use of abbreviations	Some minor errors; some correct use of abbreviations	Many errors; incorrect use of abbreviations	Numerous errors; no use of abbreviations

Rubric	4	3	2	1
Focus/Ideas	Clear, focused limerick	Most details in limerick are clear	Some details in limerick unclear	Limerick lacks clarity and development
Organization	Correct use of limerick structure	Mostly correct use of the limerick structure	Some attempt to use limerick structure	No attempt to use limerick structure
Voice	Engaged, lively voice throughout	Writer engaged with topic	Writer not very engaged	Uninterested tone
Word Choice	Strong use of sensory details	Adequate use of sensory details	Weak use of sensory details	No use of sensory details
Sentences	Energetic; tied cleverly by rhythm and rhyme	Good balance between structure and rhyme scheme	Simple but mostly connected by rhyme	Simple, error-filled; confused
Conventions	Few, if any, errors; correct use of abbreviations	Several minor errors; mostly correct use of abbreviations	Many errors; incorrect use of abbreviations	Numerous errors; no use of abbreviations

Rubric	6	5	4	3	2	1
Focus/Ideas	Clear focus and description of a person, place, or thing	Mostly clear focus and description of a person, place, or thing	Adequate focus and description of a person, place, or thing	Somewhat unfocused description of a person, place, or thing	No focus on a person, place, or thing	No understanding of description of a person, place, or thing
Organization	Clear main idea; strong use of details	Mostly clear main idea; good use of details	Adequate main idea and use of details	Attempt at main idea; somewhat unclear use of details	No main idea; unclear use of details	No attempt at main idea; no organization of details
Voice	Writer is clearly interested in what is being described	Writer shows interest in what is being described	Some interest in what is being described	Tries to show interest in what is being described	Little evidence of interest in what is being described	No interest in what is being described
Word Choice	Strong use of vivid words that appeal to the senses	Good use of vivid words that appeal to the senses	Adequate use of vivid words that appeal to the senses	Attempt to use vivid words	Little attempt to use vivid words; descriptions do not appeal to the senses	Incorrect or limited word choice; no detailed descriptions
Sentences	Clear sentences of various lengths and types	Most sentences of various lengths and types	Some variety in sentence lengths and types	Sentences of a few lengths and types	Little attempt at various lengths and types of sentences	No attempt at various lengths and types of sentences
Conventions	Few or no errors; all short sentences combined; correct use of commas	Few minor errors; most short sentences combined; mostly correct use of commas	Some minor errors; some short sentences combined; fair use of commas	Several minor errors; few short sentences combined; weak use of commas	Many errors; no short sentences combined; incorrect use of commas	Numerous errors; no short sentences combined; no use of commas

Rubric	5	4	3	2	1
Focus/Ideas	Clear focus and description of a person, place, or thing	Mostly clear focus and description of a person, place, or thing	Adequate focus and description of a person, place, or thing	No focus on a person, place, or thing	No understanding of description of a person, place, or thing
Organization	Clear main idea; strong use of details	Mostly clear main idea; good use of details	Adequate main idea and use of details	No main idea; unclear use of details	No attempt at main idea; no organization of details
Voice	Writer is clearly interested in what is being described	Writer shows interest in what is being described	Some interest in what is being described	Little evidence of interest in what is being described	No interest in what is being described
Word Choice	Strong use of vivid words that appeal to the senses	Good use of vivid words that appeal to the senses	Adequate use of vivid words that appeal to the senses	Little attempt to use vivid words; descriptions do not appeal to the senses	Incorrect or limited word choice; no detailed descriptions
Sentences	Clear sentences of various lengths and types	Most sentences of various lengths and types	Some variety in sentence lengths and types	Little attempt at various lengths and types of sentences	No attempt at various lengths and types of sentences
Conventions	Few or no errors; all short sentences combined; correct use of commas	Few minor errors; most short sentences combined; mostly correct use of commas	Some minor errors; some short sentences combined; fair use of commas	Many errors; no short sentences combined; incorrect use of commas	Numerous errors; no short sentences combined; no use of commas

Rubric	4	3	2	1
Focus/Ideas	Clear focus and description of a person, place, or thing	Fairly clear focus and description of a person, place, or thing	No focus on a person, place, or thing	No understanding of description of a person, place, or thing
Organization	Clear main idea; strong use of details	Unclear main idea; adequate use of details	No main idea; unclear use of details	No attempt at main idea; no organization of details
Voice	Writer is clearly interested in what is being described	Some evidence of interest in what is being described	Little evidence of interest in what is being described	No interest in what is being described
Word Choice	Strong use of vivid words that appeal to the senses	Some vivid words that appeal to the senses	Little attempt to use vivid words; descriptions do not appeal to the senses	Incorrect or limited word choice; no detailed descriptions
Sentences	Clear sentences of various lengths and types	Sentences of a few lengths and types	Little attempt at various lengths and types of sentences	No attempt at various lengths and types of sentences
Conventions	Few or no errors; all short sentences combined; correct use of commas	Several minor errors; most short sentences are combined; fair use of commas	Many errors; few short sentences combined; weak use of commas	Numerous errors; no short sentences combined; no use of commas

COMIC BOOK

Rubric	6	5	4	3	2	1
Focus/Ideas	Has clear plot focus; well-developed setting and characters	Mostly clear plot focus; developed setting and characters	Adequate plot and focus; adequate setting and characters	Has plot and some focus; has a setting and characters	Lacks plot and focus; poorly developed setting and characters	No plot; no focus; lacks plausible setting and characters
Organization	Correct use of comic book format	Mostly correct use of comic book format	Use of comic book format	Attempt to use comic book format correctly	Incorrect use of comic book format	No attempt at using comic book format
Voice	Consistent voice appropriate to theme and purpose	Voice consistent and appropriate to theme and types most of the time	Voice consistent and adequately appropriate to theme and types	Voice somewhat consistent and appropriate to theme and purpose	Inconsistent voice or voice inappropriate to theme and purpose	No attempt to create voice
Word Choice	Clear, concise character dialogue; reveals character traits; describes action	Adequate character dialogue; reveals most character traits; describes most action	Accurate character dialogue; reveals some character traits; describes some action	Somewhat coherent dialogue; reveals little character traits; describes little action	Flat, unclear dialogue; does not reveal character; does not describe action	No attempt to create coherent dialogue
Sentences	Clear sentences of various lengths and types	Most sentences are various lengths and types	Some sentences are various lengths and types	Sentences of a few lengths and types	Sentences of similar length and type	No attempt at sentences of various lengths and types
Conventions	Few, if any, errors; correct use of commas	Few minor errors; mostly correct use of commas	Some minor errors; adequate use of commas	Several minor errors; weak use of commas	Many errors; incorrect use of commas	Numerous errors; no or incorrect use of commas

Rubric	5	4	3	2	1
Focus/Ideas	Has clear plot focus; well-developed setting and characters	Mostly clear plot focus; developed setting and characters	Adequate plot and focus; adequate setting and characters	Lacks plot and focus; poorly developed setting and characters	No plot; no focus; lacks plausible setting and characters
Organization	Correct use of comic book format	Mostly correct use of comic book format	Use of comic book format	Incorrect use of comic book format	No attempt at using comic book format
Voice	Consistent voice appropriate to theme and purpose	Voice consistent and appropriate to theme and types most of the time	Voice consistent and adequately appropriate to theme and types	Inconsistent voice or voice inappropriate to theme and purpose	No attempt to create voice
Word Choice	Clear, concise character dialogue; reveals character traits; describes action	Mostly clear character dialogue; reveals most character traits; describes most action	Somewhat coherent dialogue; reveals some character traits; describes some action	Flat, unclear dialogue; does not reveal character; does not describe action	No attempt to create coherent dialogue
Sentences	Clear sentences of various lengths and types	Most sentences are various lengths and types	Some sentences are various lengths and types	Sentences of similar length and type	No attempt at sentences of various lengths and types
Conventions	Few, if any, errors; correct use of commas	Few minor errors; mostly correct use of commas	Some minor errors; adequate use of commas	Many errors; incorrect use of commas	Numerous errors; no or incorrect use of commas

Rubric	4	3	2	1
Focus/Ideas	Has clear plot focus; well-developed setting and characters	Has plot and some focus; has a setting and characters	Lacks plot and focus; poorly developed setting and characters	No plot; no focus; lacks plausible setting and characters
Organization	Correct use of comic book format	Use of comic book format	Incorrect use of comic book format	No attempt at using comic book format
Voice	Consistent voice appropriate to theme and purpose	Voice somewhat consistent and appropriate to theme and purpose	Inconsistent voice or voice inappropriate to theme and purpose	No attempt to create voice
Word Choice	Clear, concise character dialogue; reveals character traits; describes action	Somewhat clear dialogue; reveals some character traits; describes some action	Flat, unclear dialogue; does not reveal character; does not describe action	No attempt to create coherent dialogue
Sentences	Clear sentences of various lengths and types	Sentences of a few lengths and types	Sentences of similar length and type	No attempt at sentences of various lengths and types
Conventions	Few, if any, errors; correct use of commas	Several minor errors; mostly correct use of commas	Many errors; incorrect use of commas	Numerous errors; no or incorrect use of commas

HISTORICAL FICTION

Rubric	6	5	4	3	2	1
Focus/Ideas	Exciting story with interesting characters; historical time period and figures	Good story with developed characters; historical time period and figures	Reasonably good story; mostly based historical time period and figures	Story has some focus on characters; somewhat based on historical time period and figures	Story has some focus on characters; setting and characters are only loosely historical	Story has no focus on characters; not set in historical time period
Organization	Clear order of events	Mostly clear order of events	Can follow order of events	Order of events logical with some lapses	Unclear order of events	No order of events
Voice	Writer shows interest in the story and the characters	Writer mostly interested in the story and the characters	Writer shows reasonable interest in the story and the characters	Writer shows some interest in the story and the character	Writer is not interested in the story or characters	Writer makes no effort to show interest in the story or characters
Word Choice	Strong use of specific adjectives to bring the story to life	Good use of specific adjectives to bring the story to life	Adequate use of specific adjectives to bring the story to life	Good try at using specific adjectives; descriptions are somewhat dull	Poor use of specific adjectives; descriptions are dull	No effort made to use specific adjectives
Sentences	Strong concluding statement	Concluding statement	Adequate concluding statement	Concluding statement somewhat weak	Weak concluding statement	No clear concluding statement
Conventions	Few, if any, errors; correct use of quotation marks and parentheses	Few minor errors; mostly correct use of quotation marks and parentheses	Some minor errors; adequate use of quotation marks and parentheses	Several minor errors; little use of quotation marks and parentheses	Many errors; weak use of quotation marks and parentheses	Many serious errors; incorrect or no use of quotation marks and parentheses

Rubric	5	4	3	2	1
Focus/Ideas	Exciting story with interesting characters; historical time period and figures	Good story with developed characters; historical time period and figures	Reasonably good story; mostly based historical time period and figures	Story has some focus on characters; setting and characters are only loosely historical	Story has no focus on characters; not set in historical time period
Organization	Clear order of events	Mostly clear order of events	Can follow order of events	Unclear order of events	No order of events
Voice	Writer shows interest in the story and the characters	Writer mostly interested in the story and the characters	Writer shows reasonable interest in the story and the characters	Writer is not interested in the story or characters	Writer makes no effort to show interest in the story or characters
Word Choice	Strong use of specific adjectives to bring the story to life	Good use of specific adjectives to bring the story to life	Adequate use of specific adjectives to bring the story to life	Poor use of specific adjectives; descriptions are dull	No effort made to use specific adjectives
Sentences	Strong concluding statement	Concluding statement	Adequate concluding statement	Weak concluding statement	No clear concluding statement
Conventions	Few, if any, errors; correct use of quotation marks and parentheses	Few minor errors; mostly correct use of quotation marks and parentheses	Some minor errors; adequate use of quotation marks and parentheses	Many errors; weak use of quotation marks and parentheses	Many serious errors; incorrect or no use of quotation marks and parentheses

Rubric	4	3	2	1
Focus/Ideas	Exciting story with interesting characters; historical time period and figures	Good story with developed characters; somewhat based on historical time period and figures	Story has some focus on characters; setting and characters are only loosely historical	Story has no focus on characters; not set in historical time period
Organization	Clear order of events	Can follow order of events	Unclear order of events	No order of events
Voice	Writer shows interest in the story and the characters	Writer shows some interest in the story and the characters	Writer is not interested in the story or characters	Writer makes no effort to show interest in the story or characters
Word Choice	Strong use of specific adjectives to bring the story to life	Good try at using specific adjectives	Poor use of specific adjectives; descriptions are dull	No effort made to use specific adjectives
Sentences	Strong concluding statement	Concluding statement	Weak concluding statement	No clear concluding statement
Conventions	Few, if any, errors; correct use of quotation marks and parentheses	Several minor errors; use of quotation marks and parentheses	Many errors; weak use of quotation marks and parentheses	Many serious errors; incorrect or no use of quotation marks and parentheses